The Up South

COOKBOOK

CHASING DIXIE
IN A BROOKLYN KITCHEN

NICOLE A. TAYLOR

THE COUNTRYMAN PRESS
A division of W. W. Norton & Company
Independent Publishers Since 1923

The Countryman Press
www.countrymanpress.com

A division of W. W. Norton & Company
500 Fifth Avenue, New York, NY 10110
www.wwnorton.com

For information about special discounts for bulk purchases, please contact
W. W. Norton Special Sales at specialsales@wwnorton.com or 800-233-4830

Printed in the United States of America

Library of Congress Cataloging-in-Publication Data
Taylor, Nicole A.
The up South cookbook : chasing Dixie in a Brooklyn kitchen / Nicole A. Taylor.
    pages cm
Includes index.
ISBN 978-1-58157-301-5 (hardcover)
1. Cooking, American—Southern style. 2. Cooking—New York (State)—New York.
I. Title.
TX715.2.S68T3925 2015
641.59747—dc23

                                                                2015018282

10 9 8 7 6 5 4 3 2 1

Dedication

To

My true love and constant inspiration, Adrian Ali Franks

and

My family in Athens, Georgia, who showed me that hard work, pride, and sacrifice endures through all generations.

Contents

Foreword

I vividly remember my first meeting with Nicole Taylor. It was at Heritage Radio Network where her show—*Hot Grease*—was a major hit. She approached me with all of the energy and ardor of youth, declared that she had been "stalking" me, and began to talk about her projects. Her enthusiasm was contagious. Nicole's drawl reminded me of the soft, sibilant accents of my parents' friends of long ago. And I was struck that her Up South vividly mirrored the preserved-in-amber South in the North in which I'd been raised in the 1950s. We began to see each other, and soon she and Adrian, her husband, had become a vital part of my extended family.

Over the years of our friendship, I've learned that she has a passion for Southern food and her native Athens, Georgia that is unmatched. She also possesses an exacting eye, and she has the tenacity of a terrier when it comes to researching! She's an uncompromising cook who will search far and wide for just the right ingredient, and she is a consummate hostess who brings all of the glories of Southern hospitality to Brooklyn. As a networker, she's unsurpassed and she loves nothing better than a good tale, a good time, and a good meal.

The Up South Cookbook, which you now hold in your hands, is the sum total of all that is Nicole. In it you will meet her family and her friends through their tastes and their tales. You will be introduced to her great uncle Ben Taylor, a pillar of the church who was noted for his annual fish fry. You will become acquainted with her friend and natural hair guru, Anu Prestonia, who doesn't like to have her foods touch on her plate. You'll learn of restaurants and markets long gone like Wilfong's, her childhood fish market, and the now-defunct A&A Bakery, both in Athens, Georgia. And you will discover places that serve up foods that she has adopted in her northern home, like Russ & Daughters in NYC where she picks up smoked trout for her Smoked Trout Deviled Eggs. You'll also discover, or become reacquainted with, traditional Southern ingredients like crowder peas and butter beans, benne seeds, pokeweed, Budwine, and sorghum molasses.

The Up South Cookbook is a book to sit a spell with and savor. It's one that will end up having its pages underlined and spattered with oil. It's a book that will become a friend, and as such it will bring you the tales and tastes of Nicole Taylor as she's experienced life "chasin' Dixie" both down and Up South.

—Jessica B. Harris

Introduction

Huge pecan trees that live to be three hundred years old. Their thick trunks tell the time and hold long lost memories. Fallen nutshells crack underfoot. Whole nuts scattered in the shade. Wide-open fields full of food for the soul. Still lakes and slow-moving rivers. You want to fish? Not that river. Someone had an accident and the car fell in, drowning everyone inside. Where I'm from, a story is ready to be told and there is always sweet tea chilling and mulberries dancing in the wind. I was everybody's child. Aunts, uncles, mama, and cousins were one and the same. There was always a feast or Sunday dinner to feed aplenty. See and repeat; I don't remember ever being taught to cook anything—my eyes were useful tools. After a million glances of icing being applied with a case knife or labor-ridden hands snapping beans, I could re-create dishes.

All my journal entries from my early twenties clearly state this desire—often. I ain't country! Don't wanna be country! Don't call me country! After college, I buried almost all my food memories and replaced them with the flavor of Atlanta's hottest new restaurants—add swine and beef to the coffin. Similar to Easter, the food of my youth only rose once or twice per year. In the city, too busy to hate, I re-engaged my taste buds with the occasional trek to Busy Bee Cafe. Sitting next to the bus driver holding a sweating white Styrofoam cup and the college provost finishing off golden fried whiting gave me balance from months of eating everything but Southern food.

As a daughter of the Peach State, I was shown that offering a glass of water and piping hot edibles earned you a crown. I became a queen and a walking gastronomic encyclopedia. All my friends labeled my abode the place where modern entertaining and good eating never divorced. Then it happened: I left behind the all-day brunches and impromptu picnics in the park. I moved up, up as in Brooklyn, New York.

Seems like yesterday, I walked the longest four blocks of my life from the Nostrand Avenue A train to my new apartment in the Bedford-Stuyvesant neighborhood of Brooklyn. Passing a Golden Krust, Kentucky Fried Chicken, one-dollar pizza joints, and fruit stands selling

Caribbean specialties, everything about my new place reminded me of the West End (a tight-knit neighborhood in Atlanta). Just like that, my dream came true—but the transition wasn't smooth. Immediately, I had opinions: The fridge was too small and the bathtub had this crazy sliding glass door that gave me visions of a trapped character in a scary movie. My first few days in central Brooklyn were more like a vacation with lost luggage.

Home is supposed to have full cabinets with Carolina rice, nuts, and canned salmon—and I was starting from scratch. The movers arrived, and the square boxes of Publix Super Market's brand of dried pasta soothed my yearning for something familiar. Shopping at Fairway Market in the Red Hook neighborhood of Brooklyn was an event—rain, bus, and cab, and a fourth-floor walk-up apartment. I can't recall my grocery list or toiling in the kitchen because it was the ides of July and my feet hurt like hell. I was a wet-behind-the-ears Southern expat in a place that mocked my voice. I was sad but didn't express that emotion because I was built to adapt.

Within days of moving furniture in, I was grateful and excited about gigging for an open-space and parks nonprofit in Manhattan. I spent my breaks and downtime connecting with foodies on Twitter. The 140-character social network was a newborn, and it became the place to escape from the work I loved (but wasn't in love with). I recall my enthusiasm to be on kitchen duty, which meant cleaning the mini fridge and being responsible for the office birthday cupcakes—oh, the little things.

The stars were aligning: the rise of tres chic Brooklyn and my friendly connections with passionate gastronomes. Then I read an e-newsletter announcing Heritage Radio Network (a food culture radio station in the garden of Roberta's pizza restaurant). Days later I pitched *Hot Grease* and began hosting a weekly program dedicated to reclaiming culinary traditions, celebrations, cooking at home, and eating as a political act. Ears all over the country listened to the connections between the American South and their local food.

Memories of sitting in the kitchen and forgotten youthful friends were flooding my thoughts every second I cooked a meal. Chasing Dixie perfection brought back pig and red meat to my diet. Thanksgivings became my big test; I challenged myself to prepare a feast that screamed home. My taste testers—a group of Southerners who have made Yankee land their home. Between the loud talking and quiet bites, I began to understand that birthing a meal and saying grace with my Southern drawl connected me to the tree limbs of my being. Reflecting, the transition north breathed life into the words I wrote almost fifteen years ago, through welcoming rank strangers at my makeshift Southern Food Film Night or toasting the brightest in the emerging Brooklyn food world. I'm reminded of the Harlem Renaissance and the great migrations, when thousands of creatives arrived in droves with musical instruments, pens, paper, and antebellum taste buds, all connected to their roots but focused on an elevated life.

Up South Pantry

Southerners living above the Mason-Dixon Line understand that our foods are nuanced, that cuisines vary from Richmond, Virginia, to Athens, Georgia—that there is no definitive South. There are traditional foods of Dixie that have never touched my lips. I'm still learning the cultural plate of the Appalachian region and remain a bit confused about boiled dressing. What I know well are memorable aromas of red clay living and eating. I know that the key to mastering Southern-style cooking means incorporating flavor. I know that a pot of greens needs smokiness.

The nooks and crannies of Brooklyn inspired me to build a new pantry. Shelves with a clear vantage point of home, mixed with the spirit of New York City. Many of my ingredient-hunting adventures led to long-winded conversations explaining honeysuckles and field peas. The recipes in this book might include fish you have never heard of or wild berries you've passed by a million times. Here's a peek inside my pantry. Take a look before stocking yours:

Cellar Vegetables
Garlic
Sweet potatoes
Rutabagas
Vidalia onions
Potatoes
Turnips root
Hubbard squash or small pumpkin
White onions
Carrots
Beets
Cabbage
Leeks
Celery

Peas and Beans
Speckled butter beans
Field peas
Lima beans
Purple hull beans
Crowder peas
Sea Island red peas
Navy beans

Fruits
Pears
Apples
Mulberries
Strawberries
Quince

Concord grapes
Watermelon
Crab apples
Cherries (fresh and dried)
Lemons
Limes
Oranges
Peaches (fresh and dried)
Bananas
Pineapple
Nectarines
Blackberries
Plums
Blueberries

Vegetables
Collard greens
Mustard greens
Turnip greens
Corn
Ramps
Fresh ginger
Green tomatoes
Red tomatoes
Tomatillos
Poke salad
Dandelion greens
Yellow squash
Spring onions
Bell peppers, red and green
Jalapeños
Pole beans
Okra
Swiss chard
Mushrooms
Lacinato kale
Zucchini
Bok choy
Asparagus
Cucumber
Fennel

Flowers
Chamomile (fresh and dried)
Hibiscus (dried)
Honeysuckle (fresh and dried)
Roses (fresh and dried)

Oils
Sun Coco
Pecan
Pumpkin seed
Peanut
Olive
Sunflower
Sesame
Lard
Coconut

Vinegars and Mixtures
Angostura bitters
White vinegar
Balsamic vinegar
Apple cider vinegar
Rice vinegar
Soy sauce
Kecap manis
Black walnut bitters

Flours and Grains
All-purpose flour
Benne flour
Peanut
Pecan
Cornmeal
Grits and rice grits
Rice: Carolina Gold, wild
Popcorn
Buckwheat flour
Elbow pasta
Penne pasta

Nuts and Seeds
Peanuts
Peanut butter
Pecans
Brazil nuts
Black walnuts
Hazelnuts
Macadamia nuts
Benne seeds
Brazilian nuts

Dairy
Buttermilk
Butter
Eggs
Crème fraîche
Sour cream
Soft, hard, and fresh cheeses
Greek yogurt
Heavy cream
Half-and-half

Fresh Herbs
Sage
Chives
Parsley
Bay leaves
Thyme

Meats and Fish
Smoked ham hocks
Smoked pork neck bones
Smoked turkey necks
Smoked trout
Crappies, bream, porgies, catfish
Soft-shell crabs
Fatback
Leaf lard
Bacon
Beef
Whole duck

Chicken
Catfish
Chicken livers
Canned salmon
Pork spare ribs
Ham steak
Venison
Beef liver
Pork shoulder
Bone-in pork chops
Pork cracklings

Stocks
Chicken stock
Corn stock
Pork stock
Vegetable stock

Sugars and Aids
Light brown sugar
Dark brown sugar
Turbinado sugar
Granulated sugar
Corn syrup
Vanilla paste
Sorghum molasses
Honey
Coconut chips
Cocoa nibs
Baking powder
Cocoa powder
Baking soda
Active dry yeast
Powdered sugar
Cream of tartar
Cocoa powder
Red gel food coloring

Dark chocolate
Cornstarch

Spices
Nutmeg
Onion powder
Cumin
Ground yellow mustard, whole
    mustard seeds
Cinnamon
Garlic powder
Ground ginger
Smoked paprika
Ground tumeric
Ground white pepper
Poppy seeds
Vanilla paste
Allspice
Orange chili paste/yuzu kosho
Chile paste/sambal
Black peppercorns
Chili powder
Fennel seeds
Cardamom
Coarse salt
Black pepper
Red pepper flakes
Liquid smoke

Liquids
Coffee
Coconut milk
Cherry soda
Red wine
Dark and white rum
American whiskey

Pots and Pans
6 × 9¾-inch loaf pan
7 × 11-inch glass Pyrex casserole
12 × 17½-inch baking/jelly roll
    sheet pan
9-inch cake pan
9-inch springform pan
9-inch pie pan
10-inch Bundt pan
⅝-quart butter saucier
3½-quart All-Clad saucepan
5½-quart Le Creuset Dutch oven
12-quart stockpot
8-inch and 12-inch All-Clad skillets
12-inch and 8-inch cast-iron skillets
12-inch T-fal skillet

Miscellany
Cooling rack for baking/jelly roll
    sheets
Bowls
Grill pans
Box grater
Pie weights
Jigger
Boston shaker
Bar spoon
Bar strainer
Paring knife
Bread knife
Chef knife
Stand mixer
Blender
Belgian waffle maker

Grits and Rice

Southern saying: "Don't bite the hands that feed you."

My mother is about 5 feet tall and had a skinny frame most of my life. She hates grits, but it is nothing for her to cook a vat of grits and a small pot of rice for you. As a youngster, I mimicked her eating habits, but luckily I adore a bowl of buttery white gold.

In Brooklyn, buying stone-ground grits can be a task and is sometimes expensive. Mostly, I order online from Anson Mills, a South Carolina-based company committed to the heirloom grains once grown on coastal Georgia and South Carolina. Every blue moon, I find grit producers Nora Mill Granary and Geechie Boy Mill in specialty northeastern stores. And no visit to Athens, Georgia is complete without buying a bag of Mills Farms Red Mule Grits.

Grits

I've heard folks say, "feed that baby some grits." The mama puts the spoon in the bowl and cools the grits with short, soft blows. The first food of Southern wee ones. From packaged instant cheese to expensive stone-ground, mastering a mess of grits is a rite of passage. I've been eating grits for a long time and love the appearance to be a bit loose. Nowadays, I add whatever stock I have on hand for a fuller flavor, but using all water is fine.

Feeds 4–6

1 cup corn stock

3 cups water, plus 1 cup (optional)

2 teaspoons coarse salt

1 cup stone-ground grits

4 tablespoons unsalted butter

½ teaspoon ground black pepper

Place stock, 3 cups water, and salt in heavy medium saucepan with a lid, over high heat. Bring to a boil.

Slowly sprinkle grits into boiling water. Cover grits, reduce to low heat, and stir frequently. Sprinkling grits into boiling water prevents lumps.

Boil. . . . Sprinkle. . . . Stir.

If grits become too thick, slowly add optional cup of water to saucepan. Adjust additional water based on desired consistency.

The grits should be creamy, about 20 minutes into cooking. Add butter. Place on low heat and cook for 10 more minutes.

Remove from heat and serve hot.

Season to taste with black pepper, more salt, and butter.

Note: Don't confuse grits and polenta. Both are made from corn but from different varieties. Typically, grits have a heartier texture than their Italian cousin.

Rice

People can screw up a pot of rice. Overcooking equals a pile of mushy grains. There are a million methods to achieving perfectly done rice, including oven finishing and rinsing after cooking. This is my method.

Feeds 6

3 cups water
1 cup vegetable stock
2 teaspoons coarse salt
2 cups rice

Place water, stock, and salt in medium saucepan with a lid, over high heat. Bring to a rapid boil.

Slowly stir rice into boiling water. Cover and reduce to medium-low heat. Cook for 20 minutes without uncovering or stirring.

Remove pan from heat.

Uncover rice and let rest 5 minutes. Fluff with a fork.

Takedown Grits

"Wait, I'll be cooking hot grits in the blazing sun?" I missed the memo from the popular Takedown cooking competition held in the Dumbo neighborhood of Brooklyn. "Tell me this is a joke." Needless to say, I kept my cool, and as the NYC Food Film Festival screened *It's Grits!*, I stirred—and received an honorable mention for the simplicity and authenticity of my cheese grits topped with pork shoulder. I use cheeses from my favorite cheese makers, but many substitutions work.

Feeds 4–6

1 cup corn stock

3 cups water, plus 1 cup (optional)

2 teaspoons coarse salt

1 cup stone-ground grits

4 tablespoons unsalted butter

1 cup shredded sharp white cheddar cheese (about ¼ pound)

⅓ cup crumbled blue cheese (about 3 ounces)

½ teaspoon black pepper

Place stock, 3 cups water, and salt in heavy medium saucepan with a lid, over high heat. Bring to a boil.

Slowly sprinkle grits into boiling water. Cover grits, reduce to low heat, and stir frequently.

If grits become too thick, slowly add optional cup of water to saucepan. Adjust water based on desired consistency.

The grits should be creamy, about 20 minutes into cooking. Add butter. Stir the cheddar and blue cheese into grits. Place on low heat and cook for 10 more minutes.

Remove from heat and serve hot.

Season to taste with black pepper, more salt, and butter.

Baked Grits and Fresh Chives

A dear friend of mine is a member of an Atlanta-area Junior League Chapter, and we often joke about the organization's love for casseroles. Generally, I'm not the girl interested in the mystery mix under a pile of cheese, but every fine lady must have a deep-dish recipe. The individual ramekins and dainty chive flowers give this baked dish a modern flair.

Feeds 8

1 cup vegetable stock

3 cups water

1 teaspoon coarse salt

1 cup stone-ground grits

4 tablespoons unsalted butter, plus
    1 teaspoon to coat ramekins

¼ teaspoon ground black pepper

1 cup goat cheese (about ¼ pound)

¼ cup chopped chives

10 large eggs

Chive flowers (optional)

Preheat oven to 375°F.

Place stock, water, and salt in heavy medium saucepan with a lid, over high heat. Bring to a boil.

Slowly sprinkle grits into boiling water. Cover grits, reduce to medium-low heat, and stir frequently.

The grits should be creamy, about 20 minutes into cooking. Add butter and cook for 10 more minutes.

Turn off the heat and mix in the black pepper, goat cheese, and chopped chives. Lightly beat two eggs and stir into the grits.

Rub butter into eight ramekins. Evenly divide the grits into ramekins. Carefully crack an egg into each ramekin and bake until whites are almost set, about 12 minutes. Another option is to place the

grits in an 11 × 7-inch casserole pan and crack the eggs right on top.

Garnish with chive flowers.

Set aside. Let cool 5 minutes, then serve.

Squash and Tomatillo Grits

Indian summers and football game tailgating mark fall time in the South. My Kings County kitchen knows autumn is here when vibrant shades of squash fill our faux Saarinen kitchen table. I take great pleasure in the gray color of the Hubbard squash, a New England variety. I first bought the Yoda-looking vegetable on Martha's Vineyard at the West Tisbury Farmers' Market.

Feeds 4–6

8 cups peeled and cubed Hubbard squash
    (about 2 pounds)
2 teaspoons salt, divided
¾ teaspoon fresh sage
1 tablespoon pumpkin seed oil
1 cup halved fresh tomatillos (about ¾ of
    a pound)
3 garlic cloves, peeled and sliced
⅓ whole jalapeño, seeded
1 tablespoon lime juice (about ½ lime)
1 teaspoon coarse salt
1 cup vegetable stock
1 cup water, plus 1 cup (optional)
½ cup stone-ground grits
2 tablespoons unsalted butter
¼ teaspoon ground black pepper
Pickled onions (optional, see page 191 for
    recipe)

Preheat the oven to 350°F.

Combine the squash, 1 teaspoon salt, sage, and oil on a baking sheet. Roast for one hour, until the squash is tender.

Transfer squash to food processor or Vitamix. Purée squash until smooth. Set aside one cup of purée for the grits. The remaining squash purée can be frozen for a few weeks and used for savory pies.

Remove the husks from tomatillos. Rinse off stickiness and cut in half.

Drop tomatillos, garlic, jalapeño, lime, and salt into a food processor or Vitamix. Purée until smooth. Set aside.

Place stock, 1 cup water, and tomatillo mixture into heavy medium saucepan with a lid, over high heat. Bring to a boil.

Very slowly sprinkle grits into boiling mixture. Cover grits, reduce to low heat, and stir frequently. If grits become too thick, slowly add optional cup of water to saucepan. Adjust water based on desired consistency.

The grits should be creamy, about 20 minutes into cooking. Add butter and puréed squash.

Place on low heat and cook for 10 more minutes.

Remove from heat and serve hot. Season to taste with black pepper and more salt, if needed.

Garnish with pickled onions, if desired.

Note: If you can't find a Hubbard squash, the best substitution is a small pumpkin.

Also, it's fine to use the Pickled Hot Peppers (see page 193) here instead of a fresh jalapeño.

Fried Corn

I learned how to cook by watching folks in the kitchen. "Imma show you once, pay attention." Shucking corn was my first lesson. Recycled brown paper bags and my hands were the tools. I most remember the golden kernels going into a piping hot cast-iron skillet. The fatback reminds me of the stern "kitchen managers." Feel free to substitute thick-cut, high-quality bacon for the fatback.

Feeds 4–6

4 cups fresh corn (about 4 ears)
3 fatback slices, ½ inch each
½ cup water
1 tablespoon all-purpose flour
2 teaspoons granulated sugar
¼ teaspoon coarse salt
¼ teaspoon ground black pepper

Shuck about four ears of corn and cut off the cob. Set aside.

Place fatback (be sure to rinse off if using salt-cured variety) on medium heat; use a 12-inch cast-iron skillet. Frying time for the fatback is around 10 minutes or until crispy. Set aside pork fatback after reaching a brown and crispy look. Leave the oil in the skillet.

Place corn in hot oil. Once a few pieces of kernels are golden brown (about 5 minutes), add water. Sprinkle in flour and stir with a wooden spoon until it's a smooth, but not pasty, consistency. The kernels should be able to drop from the spoon; if not, add more water. Reduce to low heat and cook for 15 minutes.

Add sugar and salt, and stir occasionally for 5 minutes on low heat.

Season to taste with black pepper.

Rice and Spring Onion Cakes

Brooklyn-based Arancini Bros. inspired these rice cakes. Arancini or "little oranges" are traditional Italian street food rice balls made with risotto and various fillings. I use Anson Mills rice grits and create patties instead of balls. I prefer Parmesan, but using a regional artisanal hard cheese is fine. The spring onions and buttermilk give a zippy bite. The cakes will be more of a meal when paired with a side of something green.

Feeds 6

4 cups vegetable stock

1 tablespoon plus 1½ teaspoons coarse salt, divided

1 cup rice grits

½ cup finely chopped spring onion tops (about ¼ pound)

¼ teaspoon red pepper flakes

¼ cup buttermilk

1 large egg, whisked

½ cup grated Parmesan cheese (about ⅛ pound)

Large pinch ground black pepper

1 cup bread crumbs

4 tablespoons olive oil

Place vegetable stock and 1 tablespoon salt in heavy medium saucepan with a lid, over high heat. Bring to a rapid boil and add rice grits.

Reduce to medium-low heat and stir a few times. Cooking time is approximately 20 minutes. Remove from stove and let rice grits cool down. Transfer to a large bowl.

Combine onion tops, red pepper flakes, and 1½ teaspoons salt with cold rice. Fold in buttermilk, egg, cheese, black pepper, and bread crumbs. Place in the fridge for an hour.

Heat a 12-inch skillet over medium-high heat and add olive oil.

Gingerly scoop and pat rice into six patties. Work in small batches.

Transfer patties to hot oil. Brown each side for 4 minutes. The exterior will be crispy.

Chili Oil

A perfect olive oil substitution. A little goes a long way.

Makes ⅓ *cup*

2 whole, fresh red bird's eye chilies (any fresh chilies will work here)
⅓ cup olive oil

Cut chilies into ½-inch pieces.

Using a small saucepan, combine olive oil and peppers. Cook on medium-low heat for 8 minutes.

Take off the flame. Let cool.

Oil can be used right away, or transfer to an airtight container and store in the fridge.

Savory Grits Waffle

History says the chicken and waffles craze was invented in the late 1930s at the now-defunct Wells restaurant in Harlem, NYC. The combination is an American comfort food mainstay. This is my ode to the sweet and salty classic. If you don't own a waffle iron, I recommend Nordic Ware's Original Stovetop Belgian Waffle Maker.

Feeds 8

3 slices uncooked bacon

2 teaspoons brown sugar, packed

¾ cup water

1 cup vegetable stock

1 teaspoon coarse salt

½ cup stone-ground grits

2 tablespoons unsalted butter, plus
   2 tablespoons (melted) to coat
   waffle iron

1 teaspoon ground black pepper

1 cup fine cornmeal

¾ cup corn, fresh (about 1 ear)

¼ cup red bell pepper, chopped

½ teaspoon baking powder

½ teaspoon fresh ginger, grated

¼ cup buttermilk

2 large eggs, lightly beaten

Preheat oven to 300°F.

Sprinkle both sides of bacon with brown sugar. Line a jelly roll or baking sheet with aluminum foil. Place wire rack on top, put bacon on rack. Place in oven for 20 minutes. Remove and set aside. Crumble bacon (you should have about ¼ cup).

Place water, stock, and salt in heavy medium saucepan with a lid, over high heat. Bring to a boil.

Very slowly sprinkle grits into boiling water. Cover grits, reduce to low heat, and stir frequently.

The grits should be creamy, about 20 minutes into cooking. Add 2 tablespoons of unmelted butter and black pepper. Remove from heat.

Stir in cornmeal, corn, red pepper, bacon, baking powder, and ginger. Fold in buttermilk and beaten eggs.

continued

The mixture should fall off the spoon with a shake. Set aside.

Using a pastry brush, spread melted butter on the waffle iron. Cook waffles on high heat (refer to waffle iron instructions regarding heat monitoring). Refrain from opening the waffle iron too prematurely. The cooking time for this grit waffle using the Nordic Ware stovetop waffle iron is about 5 minutes.

The waffles should be golden brown and with a slight bounce-back texture.

Chaat Masala Popcorn

Chitra Agrawal is the owner of Brooklyn Delhi, a company specializing in achaar or Indian relish. Chitra is my go-to person on understanding the nuances of South Indian cuisine. She suggested the sour, yet spicy chaat masala to sprinkle over my stovetop popcorn. Using a nonstick pan with a vent lid makes this snack super easy. Otherwise, the lid should be slightly ajar.

Feeds 4

3 tablespoons coconut oil
½ cup popcorn kernels
2 teaspoons chaat masala
½ teaspoon coarse salt

Place the oil in a large nonstick pan, over medium heat. Add the popcorn; close the lid.

Let the popcorn pop. Shake the pot every 30 seconds or so to prevent burnt kernels. Total popping time is about 8 minutes.

Once the popping has slowed down, remove the pot from the heat.

Sprinkle on the chaat masala and salt. Shake thoroughly to evenly distribute the seasoning.

Southern Rice Pilaf

As a teenager, I spent an entire summer at Claflin College in Orangeburg, South Carolina. The Edisto River runs through the "garden city" and was once noted for rice production. The cafeteria at the college served rice with every meal and raised my awareness about the grain's history. I use wild rice here but switching out with any rice grain is fine.

Feeds 6–8

1½ cups wild rice

2 cups water

2¼ cups vegetable stock

½ tablespoon unsalted butter

⅔ cup chopped pecans

¾ cup finely chopped fresh parsley

2 garlic cloves, peeled and minced
   (about 1 teaspoon)

1 cup dried cherries

2–3 tablespoons Chili Oil (see page 31)

1 teaspoon coarse salt

Large pinch ground black pepper

Rinse the wild rice until the water runs clear, using a colander.

Combine the rice, water, stock, and butter in a heavy medium saucepan. Bring to a boil at medium-high heat. Turn the heat down to low and simmer. After 20 minutes, uncover and stir. Let cool another 20 minutes without uncovering.

Remove pan from heat. Uncover rice and let rest 5 minutes.

The rice should maintain a slightly firm texture. Drain off excess water.

Toss pecans into a 12-inch skillet, over medium heat. Shake skillet a bit to move nuts around. Toast for 10 minutes. Set aside.

Place parsley and garlic in a large mixing bowl. Add the dried cherries and chopped pecans.

In the cooled rice stir in 1 tablespoon chili oil. Taste, and if too spicy, stick with just the 1 tablespoon (heat will vary based on chilies used).

Sprinkle with salt and black pepper.

Peas and Things

Southern saying: "Dirt don't hurt, put it in your mouth and let it work."

The American South has more to offer than greasy fried fare. Field peas (sometimes called cowpeas or crowder peas) are an essential element in the story of Dixie. These legumes journeyed from Africa to the Americas. The colors are distinctive, some purple or speckled. Widely known as a crop that provides nutrients to the soil, field peas also promote health to other things in the garden.

No kitchen hacks are needed to remove crowder peas from their tightly packed pods or tools to snap the hairy giant pole beans. Sit on the porch with your bushel of goods, gossip a bit, and daydream a bunch. No making haste—patience required.

Purple Hull Pea Fritters

Many cookbooks feature black-eyed pea fritters. In West Africa, the golden fried nuggets are called Akkra. You can use almost any field pea but for an easier process, stick to peas without a thin outer covering.

Feeds 12

2½ cups fresh purple hull peas

½ whole fresh jalapeño, finely chopped (see note)

2 garlic cloves, peeled

½ cup chopped white onions (about 1 small onion)

1 cup plus 3 tablespoons unrefined coconut oil, divided

1¼ teaspoons ground cumin

1 teaspoon coarse salt

¼ teaspoon ground black pepper

⅔ cup vegetable stock

½ teaspoon smoked coarse salt

Add peas, jalapeño, garlic, onion, 3 tablespoons coconut oil, cumin, salt, pepper, and stock into a food processor or Vitamix.

Purée until thick and it takes a shake to fall off a spoon. Set aside.

Place 1 cup coconut oil in a 12-inch skillet over high heat. Insert an instant-read thermometer in the oil. When the temperature reaches 250°F, the fritters are ready for the skillet.

Using a small melon baller, carefully drop fritters in the oil (work in batches). Cook about a minute on each side or until golden brown. Remember to let the oil reach the 250°F mark before dropping in more fritters.

Transfer to jelly roll sheet with cooling rack on top. Sprinkle with smoked coarse salt.

Note: When using frozen peas/beans and time permits, defrost and drain all excess water.

It's okay to use Pickled Hot Peppers (see page 193) instead of a fresh jalapeño.

Limas and Leeks

Leeks, cream, and limas are a perfect marriage. I use pork stock to pull everything together.

Feeds 10–12

4 pieces fatback, ½-inch slices

2 cups chopped leeks (about 2 large leeks)

6 cups fresh lima beans

2 cups pork stock

2 cups water

¼ teaspoon granulated sugar

¼ cup finely chopped parsley

¼ cup heavy cream

½ teaspoon ground black pepper

¼ teaspoon coarse salt

Place fatback (be sure to rinse if using salt-cured variety) in 6-quart stockpot or Dutch oven, over medium heat. Leave the meat and fat drippings in the pot.

Cut the leeks between the green and white color divide. Pull apart and cut the green portion. Rinse very well to remove grit. Set aside for using in Vegetable Stock (see page 73).

Pull apart and rough cut the white portion of leeks. Rinse very well to remove grit. Place white of leeks in stockpot with hot fatback and drippings. Cook until soft.

Add the beans, stock, and water. Let simmer for 35 minutes and stir every 10 minutes or so.

After 35 minutes, add sugar and chopped parsley. Then, stir in cream. Let cook a bit more (about 10 minutes) or until beans are tender but not mushy.

Remove from heat and add pepper and salt.

Speckled Butter Beans and Tomatoes

Heather Watkins Jones interviewed me for her blog **The Blacker the Berry Food**, the first opportunity I had to tell my story of family and food. Devouring a bowl of these beans is the greatest reminder of sitting at our Formica kitchen table as a child. The vibrant spotted bean pairs wells with tomato broth. Ask your local farmer for bruised tomatoes for this dish.

Feeds 8–10

3½ cups whole tomatoes, scalded and skins removed or 1 (28-ounce) can crushed tomatoes

5½ cups vegetable stock

1 tablespoon plus 1 teaspoon coarse salt, divided

½ cup chopped white onion (about 1 small onion)

1 dried or fresh bay leaf

¼ teaspoon red pepper flakes

4 cups fresh speckled butter beans

1 tablespoon liquid smoke

¼ teaspoon granulated sugar

2 tablespoons unsalted butter

If using fresh tomatoes and you prefer tomatoes with no skins, you'll need to remove them.

Using a masher, crush the tomatoes. The wet mixture should only contain nickel-sized lumps.

Combine tomatoes, stock, 1 teaspoon salt, onion, bay leaf, and red pepper flakes in a stockpot or Dutch oven. Stir well. Heat flame to medium-high heat. Bring mixture to a simmer.

Pour in butter beans and reduce heat to medium. Let simmer for 35 minutes and stir every 10 minutes or so.

Finally, add liquid smoke, sugar, and butter. Let cook a bit more (about 10 minutes) or until beans are tender but not mushy.

Remove from heat and add 1 tablespoon salt.

Note: To remove tomato skins: Bring a medium saucepan of water to a rapid boil. Score the tomato bottoms with the letter X. Scald in hot water for 30 seconds and remove. Transfer to a bowl of cold water. Peel off skins.

NAT's BBQ Sauce

After tinkering with this recipe for years, I knew it was right when a night of Menu Mash-Up (a food board game) turned into a discussion about this sauce.

Makes 6 cups

3½ cups tomato purée, or 1 (28-ounce) container

1 cup water

⅔ cup sorghum molasses

½ cup white vinegar

3 tablespoons brown sugar

2 tablespoons liquid smoke

1 tablespoon honey

1 tablespoon lemon juice (about ½ lemon)

¾ teaspoon coarse salt

¾ teaspoon red pepper flakes

½ teaspoon ground black pepper

½ teaspoon ground cinnamon

½ teaspoon dried mustard

½ teaspoon ground cumin

½ teaspoon garlic powder

½ teaspoon onion powder

5 dashes Angostura bitters

¼ teaspoon ground ginger

Combine all the ingredients in a medium saucepan over medium heat.

Cover and bring to a boil. The sauce should be bubbling.

Reduce heat to low and let simmer for 20 minutes.

Cut off flame and let cool.

Transfer to an airtight container and refrigerate. It will last a month or so.

Note: Aromatic bitters are highly concentrated botanicals in a bottle. Rochester, New York–based Fee Brothers bitters and Angostura (made in Trinidad) are my go-tos. A dash adds complexity to more than cocktails.

No Can BBQ Baked Beans

My college roommate made baked beans that changed my life. I recall dots of meat, peppers, and smokiness. She used canned beans, but making a pot of navy beans and freezing half for future meals is a better plan. I use grass-fed beef, but switching out with ground turkey is fine.

Feeds 12

2 cups dried navy beans (1 pound)

12 cups water, divided

1½ cups cooked ground beef (about ½ pound)

4 cups chicken stock

1½ cups chopped green pepper (about 2 medium peppers)

1 cup chopped onion (about 2 small onions)

2 garlic cloves, minced (about 1 teaspoon)

2 cups NAT's BBQ Sauce (see page 44)

½ teaspoon coarse salt

½ teaspoon ground black pepper

1 tablespoon brown sugar, packed

4 bacon slices (optional)

Sort the dried beans for any debris or broken beans and discard. Place 8 cups of the water in a large bowl. Transfer beans to the water and let soak for 2 hours minimum, or overnight.

Drain and dump the soaking liquid.

Preheat oven to 375°F.

Grind your beef, if using whole beef chucks.

Brown ground beef, using a large skillet over medium-high heat, about 5 minutes. The meat should have a little pink color. Remove from heat and set aside.

Place beans, 4 cups water, and stock in a 5½-quart Dutch oven, over high heat. Bring to a steady boil, then reduce heat to medium. Cook for 1 hour or until tender but not mushy. Remove from heat.

Stir in beef, peppers, onion, garlic, and BBQ sauce. Sprinkle in salt and pepper. Transfer to 9 × 13-inch casserole pan.

Top with brown sugar. If using, cut bacon strips in half and lay over beans.

Let bake for 45 minutes. Let cool for a minimum of 30 minutes.

Sea Island Peas

Sapelo Island, off coastal Georgia, is only reachable by boat or ferry and consists of the Hog Hammock community. This island is home to blacks with a distinct culture connected to the slave trade, called Gullah Geechee. Music, ritual, and food traditions are the center of life. The red pea is special to the island because it has been unaltered since it was brought over from West Africa during the slave trade.

Feeds 6–8

1½ cups dried Sea Island red peas

8 cups water

3 cups pork stock

1 smoked ham hock

3 garlic cloves, sliced

1½ cups chopped onion (about 3 small onions)

1 dried or fresh bay leaf

½ teaspoon red pepper flakes

3 tablespoons fresh parsley

1 tablespoon plus 1½ teaspoons fresh thyme

2 teaspoons coarse salt

½ teaspoon granulated sugar

Sort the dried peas for any debris and discard. Place 8 cups water in a large bowl. Transfer beans to the water and let soak for 2 hours minimum, or overnight.

Drain and dump the soaking liquid.

Combine stock, ham hock, garlic, onion, bay leaf, red pepper flakes, parsley, and thyme in a stockpot or Dutch oven, over high heat. Stir well. Bring mixture to a simmer.

Pour in peas and reduce heat to medium-low.

Let simmer for 60 minutes and stir every 10 minutes or so.

Add salt and sugar, stir well.

Potatoes and Beets

I taught myself to make homemade French fries before becoming a teenager. Back then, I would use shortening and place wet potatoes in the oil. Popping and splattering proceeded. Now, I know better. Be sure to thoroughly dry the potatoes after the cold water bath. Adding beets reduces the guilt of chowing down on my favorite food.

Feeds 4–6

4 medium beets, skins on (about 2 pounds)
4 medium russet potatoes, skins on (about 2 pounds)
3 cups sunflower oil
½ teaspoon coarse salt

Using a vegetable brush, rinse and scrub grit off beets and potatoes.

Using a mandoline, slice potatoes with medium blade setting. Transfer to a large bowl of cold water. Set aside.

Using a mandoline, slice beets with medium blade setting. Set aside.

Drain potatoes from water. Use a salad spinner or kitchen towel to remove moisture from potatoes.

Place sunflower oil in a 12-inch skillet, over high heat. Insert an instant-read thermometer in oil. When the temperature reaches 325°F, the vegetables are ready for the skillet. Carefully drop one layer (half potatoes and half beets) into hot oil. Don't crowd the skillet.

Cook about 5 minutes on each side, or until golden brown. Work in batches, and remember to let the oil reach the 325°F mark before dropping more.

Transfer to metal rack and sprinkle with salt.

Zaatar Crowder Peas

After a trip to Cairo, Alexandria, and Luxor in Egypt, I arrived back in Brooklyn ready to merge Southern food and Khemit. One block off Atlantic Avenue near Court Street is where one can find many places to purchase Middle Eastern spices like zaatar and other cooking essentials from North Africa.

Feeds 2–4

4 tablespoons olive oil
2 tablespoons unsalted butter
2 cups fresh crowder peas
1 tablespoon zaatar spice
½ teaspoon coarse salt
Pickled Onions (optional, see page 191)

In a 12-inch skillet, add olive oil and butter, over medium heat. Be sure not to brown the butter.

Place peas in hot skillet and cover.

Leave the peas in covered skillet for 5 minutes.

Remove cover and continue cooking over medium heat for 5 more minutes. The peas will slightly crisp but become tender.

Toss with zaatar and salt. Let cook for 5 more minutes. Remove from heat and garnish with pickled onions.

Baked Macaroni and Cheese

Classic comfort food is mac and cheese. I am fascinated that there is more to cheese than cheddar. So fascinated that I own every seminal book about cheese, and contemplated being a cheese monger when I first moved to New York. Variety is the spice of life; every now and again I replace one sheep cheese for another, such as manchego.

Feeds 10–12

6 tablespoons unsalted butter, divided

½ cup heavy cream

2 cups half-and-half

½ teaspoon ground black pepper

¼ teaspoon red pepper flakes

¼ teaspoon ground nutmeg

¼ teaspoon ground mustard

2 teaspoons all-purpose flour

3½ cups shredded sharp cheddar cheese (about 1 pound)

1 cup shredded manchego cheese (about ¼ pound)

1 cup shredded Gruyère cheese (about ¼ pound)

8 cups water

1½ teaspoons coarse salt

1 pound elbow macaroni

2 large eggs, beaten

1 teaspoon smoked paprika

Preheat oven to 350°F. Prepare a 9 × 13-inch baking dish with 2 tablespoons butter.

In a heavy saucepan, whisk in cream, half-and-half, and 4 tablespoons butter over medium-low heat. Add black pepper, red pepper flakes, nutmeg, and mustard, and whisk in flour. Cook the mixture about 2 minutes, until there are no more flour lumps. The mixture should not be bubbling. If so, reduce heat.

Whisk in the cheddar, manchego, and Gruyère. Keep cheese sauce on low heat until ready for the baking dish.

Using a stockpot or Dutch oven, bring 8 cups of water to a boil. Sprinkle in salt. Put in the pasta and cook for about 8 minutes. The macaroni should not be mushy. Drain and transfer to prepared baking dish.

Mix the eggs well into the pasta. Next, pour cheese sauce over macaroni and stir well. Sprinkle paprika on top of macaroni and cheese.

Bake for 40 minutes, until you have a golden crust.

Let cool for 10 minutes before serving.

Rutabaga and Potato Gratin

Let's credit the Bedford-Stuyvesant CSA (community-supported agriculture) project for giving rutabaga a second chance in my life. This is the perfect root vegetable to pair with potatoes. Using a mandoline speeds up the vegetable-cutting process and aids in producing an evenly cooked dish. I make this gratin every Thanksgiving, and it is always the surprise winner.

Feeds 10–12

2 tablespoons unsalted butter

4 rutabagas (about 3½ pounds)

8 russet potatoes (about 4 pounds)

2 cups heavy cream

3 cups half-and-half

2 teaspoons coarse salt

½ teaspoon red pepper flakes

¼ teaspoon ground nutmeg

3 cups shredded Gruyère
   (about ¾ pound)

1 cup shredded white cheddar cheese
   (about ¼ pound)

1 cup bread crumbs

Preheat the oven to 350°F. Prepare a 9 × 13-inch baking dish with the butter.

Using a mandoline, slice rutabagas and potatoes. The blade should be set to medium. Set vegetables aside.

In a heavy saucepan, whisk in cream and half-and-half over medium-low heat. Add salt, red pepper flakes, and nutmeg.

Whisk in the Gruyère and cheddar. Keep cheese sauce on low heat until ready for the baking dish. The mixture should not be bubbling. If so, reduce heat.

Transfer a third of the vegetables to the prepared dish and add a third of the sauce. Repeat and end with vegetables as final layer.

Top with bread crumbs and bake for 40 minutes.

Let cool for 10 minutes before serving.

Spoil Me Potato Salad

A potato salad that doesn't need to be on ice for a prolonged period of time works well for picnics. The inaugural debut of my German-style potato salad was at the Atlanta Jazz Festival. Over the past 11 years, I've consistently added or subtracted flavors. Thanks to my fellow 'tater salad–obsessed friend Shannon Mustipher for inspiring the fennel usage.

Feeds 8–10

10 cups water, divided

2 teaspoons salt

8 medium potatoes (about 4 pounds)

1 cup fresh fennel, shaved

⅓ cup chopped spring onions (about 2 spring onions)

3 tablespoons butter

5 tablespoons olive oil

1½ teaspoons coarse salt

¼ teaspoon ground black pepper

½ teaspoon dried turmeric

1 teaspoon apple cider vinegar

3 sprigs fresh mint, torn

Using a stockpot or Dutch oven, bring water to a boil, over high heat. Sprinkle in salt.

Scrub potatoes with a vegetable brush. Cut into fourths and carefully drop in water. Cook the potatoes until you can barely stick a fork in them, about 10 minutes. You do not want the potatoes too tender.

Using a mandoline (the blade should be set to fine), shave fennel bulb and set aside. Chop the greens and whites of onions and set aside.

Drain potatoes and let cool down.

Transfer potatoes to a large bowl and mix butter, olive oil, salt, pepper, and turmeric. Add fennel, onions, vinegar, and mint. Mix all ingredients well.

Smoked Trout Deviled Eggs

Growing up in Athens, Georgia, I knew one Jewish person. I visited my first Jewish deli in the Toco Hills neighborhood of Atlanta. Then I moved to New York, and let me just say that nothing compares to the 100-year-old traditions found at Russ & Daughters, located in NYC's Lower East Side. Whenever you visit, buy the smoked trout.

Feeds 8

9 large eggs, hard-boiled (see note)
½ cup sour cream
¼ cup crème fraîche
4 ounces smoked trout (about ½ cup)
1 tablespoon lemon juice (about ½ lemon)
½ teaspoon balsamic vinegar
1 teaspoon dried mustard
¼ teaspoon red pepper flakes
¼ teaspoon coarse salt
¼ teaspoon ground black pepper
Large pinch ground turmeric (optional)

Carefully peel eggs. Cut them in half and place the yolks in a large bowl.

Add sour cream, crème fraîche, trout, lemon juice, vinegar, mustard, red pepper flakes, salt, and pepper. Mix well.

Fill the empty egg whites with egg yolk mixture using a melon baller or spoon. Another option is to use a pastry bag, or place the mixture in a far corner of a plastic storage bag. Cut the tip and squeeze in egg whites.

Dust the eggs with dried turmeric, if using.

Note: Having useless kitchen gadgets does make sense even in my small Brooklyn walk-up. Every now and again, I make a wise purchase. The Egg-Perfect Egg Timer is foolproof. If you don't have one, no worries, here is the old-school way:
Place large eggs in heavy medium saucepan, cover with cold water. Just enough water to cover, and no more. The flame should be set to high. Bring to a boil.
Place lid on saucepan. Remove from heat. Let sit for about 10 minutes.
Transfer eggs to a bowl of cold water. Carefully peel.

No Mayo Pimento Cheese

Blue Plate and Duke's mayonnaise brands grace plenty of picnic tables. However, I'm an "I eat mayo sometimes" gal, and I love experimenting with dairy to achieve the same texture as mayo but with different flavors. I'd describe mascarpone as a richer version of cream cheese and crème fraîche as sour cream's cousin.

Feeds 8

1 large red pepper or ⅓ cup finely chopped roasted red pepper

3 cups shredded extra sharp cheddar cheese (about ¾ pound)

½ cup mascarpone cheese (about 4 ounces)

1 cup crème fraîche

1 teaspoon balsamic vinegar

Small pinch ground black pepper

½ teaspoon coarse salt

Small pinch red pepper flakes

Rinse and wipe away any dirt from pepper.

Place dry pepper directly on open medium-high flame, using tongs. Turn every few minutes until the pepper is fully charred. Total roasting time is about 15 minutes.

Place the pepper into a bowl and cover with a kitchen towel for 10 minutes. This will assist in easy removal of the blackened skin.

Carefully remove the blackened skin by pinching and pulling. Discard the stem and deseed the pepper.

Finely chop the pepper, measure out ⅓ cup for the recipe. Set aside.

Store remaining chopped pepper in airtight container in refrigerator.

Combine cheeses, crème fraîche, vinegar, black pepper, salt, red pepper flakes, and chopped red pepper. Mix until all ingredients have been incorporated. I prefer a thicker spread, but if you like smooth, pop the mixture into a food processor and pulse a few times until desired texture.

Serve immediately or refrigerate.

Pole Beans with Turnips

I asked Sanura Weathers, the food blogger behind myliferunsonfood.com, to contribute an old-timey bean recipe. Without a pause she pulled this from her amazing archive.

This summer dish is served in every Southern grandparents' home. It's brought out at weddings, funerals, and special events. The sight of it makes pseudo-healthy eaters start a conversation about unhealthy Southern food. Every child of the South has memories of watching television, only to have a large bowl of raw pole beans unexpectedly placed in front of them. They dare not verbally protest. The snapping sound of wax green bean ends are heard along with the sound of the television. For a generation of a certain age, such sounds bring back memories of watching their grandparents prepare meals.

Feeds 6–8

4 tablespoons olive or safflower oil, divided

1 large turnip, peeled and cut into ½-inch chunks

1 medium sweet onion, diced

1 teaspoon sea salt, more or less to taste

1 teaspoon fresh black pepper, more or less to taste

½ teaspoon crushed red pepper, more or less to taste

2 garlic cloves, minced

2 roughly chopped smoked turkey pieces with bone and skin (about 1–1½ pounds)

Pour about 2 tablespoons of the oil in a large pot over medium-high heat. When the oil is hot, add the turnip chunks. Frequently stir until the turnips hint at turning golden brown, about 10 minutes. Remove to a paper towel–lined bowl. Place turnips aside.

If needed, add the last 2 tablespoons of oil to the pot. Stir in the onions. Season with salt, pepper, and red pepper. Frequently stir until the onion is transparent (about 5 minutes). Stir in the minced garlic for up to 20 seconds. Add the chopped turkey and stir for about 5 minutes or until thoroughly heated.

Add the broth, ¼ cup vinegar, and sugar. Cover and bring to a boil. Reduce temperature to bring the broth to a simmer. Let simmer for 15 minutes.

1 quart chicken broth/stock, more or less to barely cover green beans

½ cup apple cider, white balsamic, or pepper vinegar, more or less to taste, divided

2 teaspoons coconut or brown sugar

2 pounds wax green beans, ends trimmed and cleaned (see note)

Stir in the green beans. Cover and bring the pot to a simmer. After 30 minutes, if necessary, adjust seasoning by adding the other ¼ cup vinegar. Let simmer on low temperature for an additional 50 minutes, more or less according to personal taste or texture. Occasionally taste to adjust seasoning.

Return the turnips to the pot. Cook for an additional 10 minutes or when the turnips are fork tender. If necessary, adjust seasoning.

Ladle into individual bowls and enjoy.

Note: Use wax green beans or pole beans instead of the delicate French haricot vert.

Greens and More

Southern saying: "A pot can't call a kettle black."

There is folklore that says eating leafy greens after the 8 p.m. hour gives you crazy dreams or kills you. I remember explaining the proverb to Fany Gerson, chef/owner of Dough in Brooklyn and cookbook author, after we ate a plate full of greens in New Orleans. The truth is that cabbage and many other super foods contain a gas-producing enzyme. My guess is that the digestion makes one restless and the gas mirrors heart pain—not death.

Slow-Cooked Collard and Turnip Greens

Tearing, cleaning, and cooking greens were a Saturday night ritual. The smell of greens lingered in my Saturday clothes. A five-senses memory and a reminder to jump-start my cooking projects. If you want to unwind, skip the precut bagged varieties.

Feeds 12–14

12 cups water

3 smoked ham hocks

1½ cups chopped onions (about 1 large onion)

4 garlic cloves, smashed

1 teaspoon salt

1 teaspoon black pepper

1 pound turnip greens (about 6 cups, chopped)

2 pounds collard greens (about 12 cups, chopped)

1 tablespoon plus 1½ teaspoons apple cider vinegar

½ teaspoon sugar

Dash pepper vinegar (optional)

Place water, hocks, onions, garlic, salt, and pepper in 12-quart stockpot. Cover with lid.

Simmer on medium-low heat for at least 2 hours.

Hand trim stems of greens and set aside for later use in Collard Green Pesto and Pasta (see page 63). Tear turnip and collard leaves.

Add the leaves to stockpot and cover. The greens will wilt down. Cook for 1 hour and 30 minutes on medium-low heat. Stir from time to time.

Around the 1 hour cooking mark, pour in apple cider vinegar and sprinkle in sugar.

Transfer a heaping bowl of greens and potlikker to plate.

If you love a kick, dash a little Hot Pepper Vinegar (see page 195) on the greens.

Collards Goma-ae

I spent an afternoon cooking and experimenting with writer and cultural activist Nina Ichikawa. We chatted for hours in her sun-drenched Fort Greene neighborhood apartment about Japanese food and Southern foodways. Traditionally, Goma-ae consists of spinach.

Feeds 2–4

2 tablespoons salt

4 cups julienned collard greens (about ⅔ pound)

4 tablespoons sesame seeds

1 tablespoon rice vinegar

1½ teaspoons soy sauce

1 teaspoon granulated sugar

In a stockpot or Dutch oven, add enough water to submerge the collards and bring water to boil. Add salt to the boiling water and add the collard greens. Boil for 6 minutes.

Drain the collard greens and place the greens in a large bowl with ice water. This shocks the greens, to stop further cooking. Spin the greens in a salad spinner to remove excess water.

In a small dry skillet on medium heat, toast the sesame seeds until golden brown, about 6 minutes. Pour the toasted seeds into a mortar and crush with the pestle. Add the vinegar, soy sauce, and sugar; stir together.

Drain the collard greens and toss the dressing with the greens. Serve at room temperature with white rice.

Collard Green Pesto and Pasta

Waste not, want not. Composting can be a challenge in a small Brooklyn apartment with a less than average-sized refrigerator. If I have room, I throw scraps of vegetables in the fridge for stock. With collard greens, I make pesto from leaves and a handful of stems.

Feeds 6–8

3 cups coarsely chopped fresh collards
   (about ½ pound)

1 cup chopped pecans

1 cup grated pecorino Romano cheese
   (about 3½ ounces)

½ cup pecan oil

¼ cup olive oil

1 teaspoon honey

½ teaspoon soy sauce

¼ teaspoon sambal (chili paste)

¼ teaspoon coarse salt

Large pinch ground black pepper

4 garlic cloves, peeled

16 cups water

1 tablespoon coarse salt

1 pound linguine

Combine all ingredients through the garlic in a heavy-duty blender or food processor. Purée until smooth. This makes about 2 cups. Set aside 1 cup for the pasta and refrigerate the remaining amount for future use.

Using a stockpot or large Dutch oven, bring the water and salt to a boil. Cook the pasta until al dente, according to the pasta package instructions. Drain, reserving the pasta water.

Combine 1 cup pesto, ½ cup pasta water, and pasta in a large bowl and toss together until the pasta is fully coated. Add a bit more pasta water or pesto if you wish.

Poke Salad Frittata

Foraging is the nouveau name for picking wild edibles from one's surroundings. I grew up across from North Oconee River Park where poke salad was abundant. Poke leaves must be gathered mid-spring before the flower buds bloom. Before eating the poke-weed, the leaves must go through a few cycles of fresh, boiled water. Not interested in trekking through the woods? Replace with beet greens.

Feeds 4

3 tablespoons olive oil

2 tablespoons butter

2 cups sliced onions (about 2 large onions)

2 garlic cloves, minced (about 1 teaspoon)

4 cups poke salad or beet greens, chopped

6 large eggs, beaten

½ cup half-and-half

1½ teaspoons coarse salt

½ teaspoon ground black pepper

¼ teaspoon red pepper flakes

Preheat the oven to 325°F.

In a 12-inch nonstick skillet on medium heat, add the oil and butter. Once warm, add the onions and cook for 5–10 minutes or until lightly browned. Add the garlic and cook until fragrant, 1 minute.

Add the greens and mix together. Remove from heat.

Combine the eggs, half-and-half, and spices in a large bowl. Whisk well. Pour the egg mixture over the vegetables.

Place in the oven for 5–6 minutes, until eggs are barely set.

Remove and cool for 5 minutes.

Mustard Greens and Potato Hash

When it came to food, making do was something that was taught through action and not words. Potatoes were always in the house, and probably were one of the first things I learned to cut, peel, fry, or mash. Round and dirty, hanging from a wire basket with onions above them. This is a lazy Sunday breakfast treat. Most times, I'll add a fried or boiled egg on top. I love the spiciness of mustard greens, but any leafy green will substitute well.

Feeds 2–3

3 medium white potatoes, cubed (1 pound)
1 cup chopped onion (about 1 large onion)
1 clove garlic, minced (about ½ teaspoon)
3½ cups mustard greens (about ½ pound)
3 tablespoons olive oil
2 tablespoons unsalted butter
2 teaspoons honey
½ teaspoon coarse salt
Large pinch ground black pepper

Rinse and scrub any dirt from potatoes. Pat dry and cut into ½-inch cubes.

Cut onion and set aside. Mince garlic and set aside.

Rinse and dry mustard green leaves. Pat dry. Roll several leaves together at a time and cut vertically, until all leaves are cut. Set aside.

Add the oil and butter to a 12-inch skillet over medium-high heat. Once the butter is melted, add the potatoes. Cook the potatoes for 6 minutes, don't disturb the pan, then flip over the golden brown potatoes and fry for another 6 minutes. This ensures a crispy texture.

Add the onions and cook until softened, about 2 minutes.

Add the mustard greens to potatoes; do not toss around. Let hang on top for 5 minutes before mixing with potatoes.

Stir in honey. Add garlic.

Sprinkle with salt and pepper.

Remove from flame and serve.

Swiss Chard Rolls

Perfecting these veggie rolls has been a labor of love. Only one person understands my quest to capture the flavor of the leafy green rolls I devoured at a party at the now-closed East Atlanta Village Spa. My dear friend Stacey West remembers the moment— juicy and filling. Buy a bottle of kecap manis (caramelized soy sauce) in the Asian aisle or specialty food store for dipping.

Feeds 4

12 cups water

1 tablespoon plus ½ teaspoon coarse salt, divided

1 bunch rainbow Swiss chard

1 teaspoon sesame seeds

2 tablespoons unsalted butter

2½ cups chopped mushrooms (1 pound)

1 cup chopped spring onions (½ pound)

½ cup chopped onions (1 small onion)

½ cup chopped carrots (¼ pound)

2 cloves garlic, minced (about 1 teaspoon)

1½ teaspoons sesame oil

1 teaspoon honey

½ teaspoon rice vinegar

¼ teaspoon red pepper flakes

Kecap manis (optional)

Bring the water and 1 tablespoon of salt to a boil, using a stockpot or Dutch oven. Remove the stems from the Swiss chard and blanch for 30 seconds. Transfer to a bowl of cold water.

Transfer chard to baking sheets lined with paper towels. Set aside.

Toast the sesame seeds in a nonstick skillet on medium heat. The sesame seeds should turn a light brown color. Set aside.

Add the remaining ½ teaspoon salt, butter, mushrooms, spring onions, onions, carrots, and garlic. Cook on medium heat about 10 minutes, or until veggies are soft.

Take the pan off the heat. Pour in sesame oil, honey, rice vinegar, red pepper flakes, and toasted sesame seeds.

Position dried Swiss chard on a cutting board or flat surface and stuff about 2 tablespoons vegetable filling in the center of the leaf.

Next, tuck the sides in, fold, and roll the chard. Try to use leaves without bulky stems.

Cut in half and dip in caramelized soy sauce, also known as kecap manis, if desired.

Fried Cabbage

Remember the repurposed shortening container near the stove? We called it a grease can, because it was the place where all the bacon drippings lived. You dig out a spoonful and use it instead of butter or olive oil. I need to bring that practice back; until then I'll cook up pork fat.

Feeds 6

3 pieces fatback, ½-inch slices
4 cups shredded cabbage (about 1 head cabbage)
½ teaspoon ground black pepper
¼ teaspoon coarse salt
¼ teaspoon red pepper flakes

In a 12-inch skillet on medium heat, place the fatback into the pan (be sure to rinse off if using the salt-cured variety). Let the fatback heat while you prep the cabbage. Frying time for the fatback is about 10 minutes or until crispy.

Remove the outer leaves of cabbage. Wipe off the cabbage with a paper towel to remove any dirt (do not rinse). Cut the cabbage in half, then fourths, about 4 cups of cabbage total.

Remove the fatback from the pan. Leave the drippings in the skillet. Add the cabbage, pepper, salt, and red pepper flakes to the pan. Let cook down for 8 minutes on medium heat. Reduce heat to medium-low and cook for an additional 10 minutes, until the cabbage is more of a translucent green color.

Raw Kale, Dandelion, and Orange Salad

It's hard to believe that I was a vegetarian for 10 years. I binged on kale and dandelion around the same time swine returned to my life. Nowadays, I follow the rule of Meatless Monday, the national campaign that urges us to go meat-free one day per week.

Feeds 4–6

½ cup olive oil

¼ cup balsamic vinegar

1 tablespoon hot honey (see note)

¼ teaspoon coarse salt

¼ teaspoon ground black pepper

6 cups chopped lacinato kale (about 1 pound)

2 cups chopped dandelion greens (about ¼ pound)

¼ cup chopped peanuts

1 navel orange, segmented (see note)

⅓ cup Tomme cheese, shredded (about ⅛ pound)

In a large bowl, whisk together the olive oil, vinegar, honey, salt, and pepper. Add the kale, dandelion, and peanuts. Massage the leaves with dressing, until the leaves are evenly saturated with dressing.

Take 2 orange pieces and squeeze the juice over salad greens.

Add the remaining orange segments and shredded cheese to the bowl. Serve immediately.

Note: Can't find hot honey (chili-infused) in your 'hood? Use regular honey and a pinch of red pepper flakes.

Another way to segment an orange is to cut the peel, using a paring knife. Then, carefully cut between the white membrane. Segments will be free of the outer skin. Take the leftover mass and squeeze over salad greens.

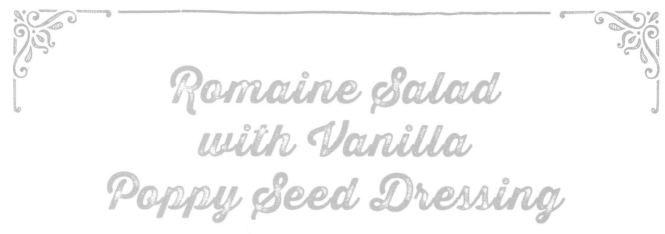

Romaine Salad with Vanilla Poppy Seed Dressing

It's a privilege to have been in the mix during the breakout time of Roberta's pizza restaurant. The year was 2009 when I joined the Heritage Radio Network. Two shipping containers were turned into a food podcasting station, located in Roberta's garden. Every visit to Roberta's, the poster child of the DIY and hipster movement, must include the romaine salad. I make this recipe when I can't brave the long wait times of this Brooklyn classic restaurant.

Feeds 4

⅓ cup Greek yogurt, full fat
¼ cup poppy seeds
1 tablespoon olive oil
2 teaspoons rice vinegar
½ teaspoon vanilla paste
½ teaspoon coarse salt
Large pinch ground white pepper
1 head romaine lettuce, whole leaves
   (about 1 pound)

Whisk together all ingredients except for the lettuce. Pour dressing over the lettuce and serve immediately.

Store any leftover dressing in refrigerator for up to one week.

Vegetable Stock

I only purchase boxed stock in a pinch. Nothing wrong with store-bought, but it makes sense for me to bag up carrot scraps, celery, and leek tops and then make stock when my freezer gets too full of them. If you don't save the veggie leftovers, feel free to ask your local farmer for bruised vegetables that you can use for stock.

Another option here is to use corn cobs, without the kernels. If doing so, use about 8 small ears and omit the other vegetables.

Makes 4½ cups

10 cups water

3 carrots, chopped rough (½ pound)

2 leeks, chopped rough (1 pound)

1 bunch celery, chopped rough (1 pound)

2 teaspoons coarse salt

1 teaspoon whole black pepper

1 tablespoon fresh parsley, chopped

1 tablespoon fresh thyme

1 dried or fresh bay leaf

Place water, carrots, leeks, celery, salt, black pepper, parsley, thyme, and bay leaf in 12-quart stockpot, over high heat. Cover with lid.

Bring all ingredients to a boil. Reduce to medium-low heat.

Simmer for three hours.

Let cool completely.

Strain and discard vegetables.

Place in freezer for several months and fridge for around 3 days.

Raw Zucchini and Yellow Squash Salad with Chamomile Dressing

Everyone in my East Athens neighborhood in Georgia had a backyard garden. My great-aunt planted one in my childhood home, and I've been begging my family to revive it. The harvest was always full of yellow squash. The idea of chamomile came from the chef/co-owner of El Rey in NYC after he gifted me fresh chamomile.

Feeds 4

1 cup hot water

¼ cup dried chamomile

2 tablespoons olive oil

1 tablespoon lime juice (from ½ lime)

1 teaspoon honey

½ teaspoon white vinegar

¼ teaspoon coarse salt

3 cups chopped squash

2 cups chopped zucchini (about 1 large)

¼ cup thinly sliced spring onions
   (¼ pound)

Bring the water to a boil, add to the chamomile, and let steep and cool for one hour. Strain through a fine-mesh strainer. Reserve 2 tablespoons for the dressing.

Combine the 2 tablespoons chamomile liquid with oil, lime juice, honey, vinegar, and salt. Whisk together.

In a large bowl, toss the squash, zucchini, and onions with the dressing. Serve immediately.

Apple and Bok Choy Salad

Deciding to veer from my standard grilled bok choy recipe was difficult. In New York City, bok choy and apples hang out at the farmers' market around the same time. This simple salad takes minutes to make. I'm always trying to find a way to sneak Southern nuts into meals.

Feeds 2

2½ cups bok choy leaves

1 cup cubed apples (about 2 small apples)

2 teaspoons lime juice (about ½ lime)

1 teaspoon pecan oil or other oil

2 tablespoons chopped salted peanuts or other nut

¼ teaspoon coarse salt

Large pinch ground black pepper

2 tablespoons blue cheese (about ½ ounce)

Place bok choy leaves and apples in a large bowl or serving platter.

Drizzle lime juice and oil on top and toss together. Sprinkle in peanuts, salt, and pepper. Toss again.

Crumble the blue cheese over the salad.

Serve immediately.

Fried Okra

"Keep living and you'll end up eating a lot of things," says my mother. Hello, okra, my new friend. You were never in my rotation but now we hang out. I like your tenderness and how you fry up.

Feeds 4

2 cups chopped okra (about 1 pound)
¾ cup buttermilk
½ teaspoon coarse salt
½ teaspoon ground black pepper
½ cup fine cornmeal
½ cup all-purpose flour
¼ teaspoon onion powder
¼ teaspoon smoked paprika
¼ teaspoon red pepper flakes
1½ cups sunflower oil

Gently rub any dirt off okra. Cut into ½-inch pieces, discard hard stem.

Pour buttermilk in a shallow bowl, add the okra and soak for 15 minutes.

Combine the salt, pepper, cornmeal, flour, onion powder, smoked paprika, and red pepper flakes in a large bowl. Whisk together well.

Toss buttermilk-soaked okra in cornmeal mixture. Using a spider strainer or slotted spoon, shake off excess cornmeal.

Place oil in a 12-inch skillet over high heat. Insert an instant-read thermometer in oil. When the temperature reaches 350°F, the okra is ready for the skillet.

Carefully drop okra in the oil (work in batches). Cook about a minute and flip over, until golden brown. Remember to let the oil reach the 350°F mark before dropping more okra, and don't crowd the pan.

Transfer to baking sheet with cooling rack on top. Sprinkle with more salt, if desired.

Let's talk okra. If you've never witnessed them growing from seed to pod, it's something beautiful. Gorgeous flowers grow right beside the vegetable and can be used to thicken soup or simply fried. The inside anatomy of okra is often used as stencils or stamps: artful food.

Vidalia Onion Dutch Baby

Being a creature of habit has its advantages. If there is a crowd over for brunch, I make Dutch babies. The one-pan German pancake requires less work than individual flapjacks. The key to this beauty is keeping a hot pan. Sweet Dutch babies can be found tucked on many restaurant menus. Here I'm all about the savory.

Feeds 4

3 tablespoons lard, or other fat or oil, divided

1½ cups sliced Vidalia or sweet onions (about 2 large onions)

¾ teaspoon coarse salt, divided

½ teaspoon brown sugar, packed

1 large pinch black pepper

4 large eggs, beaten

½ cup half-and-half

¾ cup all-purpose flour

1½ teaspoons garlic powder

Preheat the oven to 450°F.

In a 12-inch cast-iron skillet on medium-high heat, heat 2 tablespoons lard.

Add the onions, ½ teaspoon of the salt, and black pepper. Cook for about 10 minutes, until the onions are translucent. Remove the onions from the pan, setting them to the side.

Whisk together the eggs and half-and-half. Add the flour, garlic powder, and remaining ¼ teaspoon salt to the egg mixture and whisk to combine.

Grease the skillet with the remaining tablespoon of lard. Place the skillet in the oven and heat for 10 minutes.

Pull the hot pan out of the oven, pour the batter and onions into the pan, and put back into the oven. Bake for 15 minutes.

Remove from oven and serve immediately.

Note: Real-deal sweet Vidalia onions are grown in only 20 counties in the state of Georgia.

Yard Bird and Fish

Southern saying: "A closed mouth don't get fed."

Enter the vestibule, pull up a seat, and get ready for the gospel. I'm serving this to you straight up, right from the fryer. I eat my weight in chicken, and every bird isn't made the same: A friend was amused that heritage-breed turkey doesn't produce enough fat and drippings to make gravy. I prefer young chickens for all my cooking. They are small in size and young in age.

When it comes to fish, I stay clear of farm raised (with the exception of oysters and catfish). If you think everyone in the South eats shrimp and grits, au contraire. In my neck of the woods, shrimp was never around and was quite costly. The deep freezer stayed full of trout, crappies, and porgies.

Fried Chicken

My favorite saying to rattle off to my longtime friend Reginald Dye is, "You ain't no spring chicken." Reggie loves my fried chicken wings, and any hole-in-the-wall or white tablecloth with flavorful fowl. I live and die by seasoning the bird and batter. Fry up the entire chicken or just your favorite pieces.

Feeds 8–10

1 (3–4 pounds) fryer chicken, cut up

½ lemon

2 tablespoons plus 2 teaspoons coarse salt, divided

2 teaspoons ground black pepper, divided

½ teaspoon ground cinnamon

1½ cups coconut milk, unsweetened, or 1 (13½-ounce) container

½ cup buttermilk

1½ cups all-purpose flour

1 cup cornstarch

1 teaspoon red pepper flakes

1 tablespoon fresh thyme

1 teaspoon garlic powder

1 teaspoon onion powder

4 cups peanut oil or lard

Fresh flat-leaf parsley (optional)

Rinse the chicken and rub it with half a lemon (I do this to sanitize chicken). Pat dry, season with 2 tablespoons of the salt, 1 teaspoon of the pepper, and cinnamon. Place the chicken in a large bowl, cover it, and refrigerate for 30 minutes.

In a separate large bowl, combine the coconut milk, buttermilk, and chicken. Cover the chicken and refrigerate for a minimum of 30 minutes.

In a shallow dish combine flour, cornstarch, red pepper flakes, thyme, garlic powder, and onion powder. Dredge the chicken in the dry mix.

Add oil to a 12-inch cast-iron skillet on high heat. Let the oil reach 350°F, using an instant-read thermometer.

Work in batches. Temperature should hover around 350°F.

Cook wings for about 15 minutes (turn at each 5-minute mark).

Breast, thighs, and legs cook in about 25 minutes (turn at each 5-minute mark).

Chicken should look like it's almost floating.

Transfer to jelly roll pan with cooling rack on top. This keeps the skin crispy. For easy cleaning, line with pieces of brown paper bags or paper towels.

Garnish with parsley, if desired.

Chicken Liver Sliders

My mother worked at a poultry plant, processing chicken for over 30 years. My earliest memories of her cooking are tied to chicken livers. Seems like they'll be the next culinary trend; my local butcheress at Greene Grape Provisions says more folks are requesting the innards. Enjoy the livers on Martin's Potato Rolls (party size) with your favorite hot sauce. I keep Bacchanal Pepper Sauce on hand, a tropical hot condiment made in Brooklyn.

Feeds 4–6

1½ cups chicken livers (½ pound)
2 large eggs, beaten
1 teaspoon coarse salt
¼ teaspoon ground black pepper
¾ cup all-purpose flour
¼ cup cornstarch
½ teaspoon coarse salt
1½ teaspoons fresh thyme
¼ teaspoon onion powder
¼ teaspoon garlic powder
¼ teaspoon red pepper flakes
Large pinch ground black pepper
4 cups peanut oil
Fresh flat-leaf parsley (optional)

Rinse chicken livers well. Pat dry. Place in bowl of beaten eggs. Set aside.

In a shallow dish, combine all dry ingredients. Dredge the chicken in the dry mix.

Add the oil to a 12-inch cast-iron skillet, on high heat. Let the oil reach 375°F, using an instant-read thermometer.

Cook for a total of 10 minutes (5 on each side).

Garnish with parsley, if using.

Note: Purchase a splatter screen for your cast-iron skillet. The chicken livers pop a lot even after patting dry.

Grilled Whole Fish

Once upon a time, a family sat a toddler in the middle of the floor with a bone-filled piece of fish. The tiny kid meticulously picked all the bones out and ate happily ever after.

I discovered yuzu (an Asian citrus fruit) after stumbling upon Sunrise Mart in New York's Soho neighborhood. An emporium of Japanese goodness. You can use a regular orange and hot sauce to replace the yuzu and yuzukosho.

Feeds 2–4

2 whole porgies, gutted and cleaned (about 7 pounds)

½ lemon

½ tablespoon coarse salt

½ teaspoon ground black pepper

1 teaspoon The Franks seasoning (see Fish and Seafood Fry, page 89)

1 large yuzu (orange), sliced

1 tablespoon unsalted butter

1 teaspoon yuzukosho (orange chili paste)

2 teaspoons sesame oil

Preheat the oven to 350°F.

Ask your fishmonger to gut, clean, and leave the head on your fish.

Rinse the fish and pat dry. Rub with half a lemon. Season with the salt, pepper, and seasoning mix. Set aside.

Creating two foil packets, one for each fish, lay down a layer of sliced yuzu.

Add the fish, stuffing a few slices of yuzu into the cavity. Top with additional citrus slices.

Dab the butter and yuzukosho on top of each fish. Drizzle the oil and close up the foil packets.

Place in oven and bake for 45 minutes.

When ready, the fish will have a soft flake and be opaque inside.

Fish and Seafood Fry

A navy man, deacon, church treasurer, and fisherman—my great-uncle Ben Taylor. He was the last person to leave the church and if you rode home with him after services, you accompanied Mr. Taylor as he dropped the Sunday offering in the deposit drop at the bank. Every year, he held a big fish fry. All the sea meat was from his fishing trips. The Franks seasoning is named after my husband; it's my version of the popular yellow-and-red tin can spice mix used for seafood.

Feeds 4

THE FRANKS SEASONING

Makes ⅓ cup

2½ tablespoons celery salt

2 teaspoons smoked paprika

1 teaspoon ground mustard

½ teaspoon ground cinnamon

¼ teaspoon ground allspice

¼ teaspoon ground ginger

¼ teaspoon red pepper flakes

¼ teaspoon ground nutmeg

FISH

4 whole porgies (about 14 pounds)

½ lemon

1 tablespoon plus 1½ teaspoons coarse salt

1 teaspoon ground black pepper

1 tablespoon The Franks seasoning

2 large eggs, beaten

2 tablespoons water

4½ cups peanut oil

The Franks seasoning: Combine all ingredients and mix well.

Store in a small airtight container. Place in cool, dark place with other spices.

The fish and cornmeal batter: Ask your fishmonger to gut, clean, and leave the head on your fish.

Rinse the fish and pat dry. Rub with half a lemon.

Season with the salt, pepper, and seasoning mix. Set aside.

Combine the eggs and water until smooth. Pour over fish and coat well.

In a shallow dish, combine all cornmeal batter ingredients. Set aside.

Dredge fish in cornmeal batter.

Add the oil to a 12-inch cast-iron skillet or Dutch oven, on high heat. Let the oil reach 325°F, using an instant-read thermomoter.

continued

CORNMEAL BATTER

1 teaspoon red pepper flakes

2 teaspoons coarse salt

2 teaspoons The Franks seasoning

1½ cups fine cornmeal

¼ cup all-purpose flour

¼ cup cornstarch

¼ cup pecan flour

Fry the fish about 15 minutes. If using a skillet, flip fish at the 7-minute mark. Be careful of the hot oil.

Work in batches; temperature should hover around 325°F.

When ready, fish should look like it's almost floating.

Transfer to jelly roll pan with cooling rack on top. This keeps the skin crispy. For easy cleaning, line with pieces of brown paper bags or paper towels.

Note: Throw a few oysters in the fish-fry mix. If you are unsure about shucking them, ask the fishmonger to keep them on the half shell. Cooking time for oysters is about 1 minute.

Chicken Mushroom Soup with Asparagus and Ramps

Ramps are the darling of springtime. I'd never heard of this wild onion until it popped up on the menu of several of my favorite restaurants. Why not pair them with other second-quarter vegetables?

Feeds 8

2 tablespoons olive oil

2 cups asparagus bottoms (about ¾ pound), see note

⅓ cup ramp tops

3 cups sliced portabella mushrooms (about 1½ pounds)

1 cup sliced shiitake mushrooms (½ pound)

4 cups chicken stock

2 cups heavy cream

2 tablespoons unsalted butter

⅓ chopped chicken (optional)

1 tablespoon pickled ramp bottoms (garnish)

½ cup morels (optional)

Using a stockpot or large Dutch oven on medium heat, heat the oil and sauté the asparagus, ramps, and mushrooms. Cook the vegetables until softened, about 15 minutes.

Add the chicken stock and bring to a simmer. Using an immersion blender, blend until the mixture is smooth. Cook for another 25 minutes.

Stir in the heavy cream and simmer for an additional 30 minutes.

Stir in the butter and serve. Garnish with the chopped chicken, pickled ramps, and morels.

Note: I always keep the fibrous end of the asparagus and place in the freezer. Frozen asparagus bottoms are fine to use if you don't have fresh, just make sure to defrost and drain.

Whole Roasted Bird

When new home cooks seek advice about menus, I tell them to master roasting poultry. I follow these rules with chicken and Thanksgiving turkey. No brine, just butter.

Feeds 4

COMPOUND BUTTER

Makes 1 cup

¾ cup unsalted butter, softened (1½ sticks)

¼ cup chopped fresh parsley

¼ cup chopped fresh sage

1 tablespoon fresh thyme

1 teaspoon minced garlic

¼ teaspoon coarse salt

Small pinch ground black pepper

WHOLE ROASTED BIRD

1 whole chicken (4 pounds)

1 tablespoon plus 1½ teaspoons coarse salt

1½ teaspoons ground black pepper

3 whole lemons (½ pound)

½ cup roughly chopped onion (about 1 small onion)

2 tablespoons compound butter

1 tablespoon olive oil

The compound butter: Combine all ingredients in the bowl of a stand mixer or large bowl. Mix on medium speed until combined. Place the butter mixture on a sheet of wax or parchment paper and roll into a log. Freeze until solid.

The whole roasted bird: Preheat the oven to 400°F.

Rinse the chicken and pat dry with kitchen towel or paper towel.

Cut the head off, place the innards in freezer for stock or Chicken Liver Sliders (see page 86). This is only necessary if you have a "straight-from-the-farm" chicken.

Transfer chicken to a large roasting pan.

Sprinkle salt and pepper on the entire chicken, including the inside cavity. Stuff the chicken with half the lemons and onions. Arrange the remainder around the chicken.

Massage the bird with 2 tablespoons of compound butter. Drizzle olive oil over the top of bird.

Place in the oven and roast for 1 hour. Internal temperature should be around 180°F.

GRAVY

1 cup chicken drippings

½ cup vegetable stock, divided

4 tablespoons butter

4 tablespoons flour, divided

1 teaspoon fresh herbs

Small pinch coarse salt

Small pinch ground black pepper

Remove from oven and let rest for about 15 minutes before cutting.

The gravy: I use a drop cooking method when making gravy. Meaning, I eyeball the ingredients. Around these parts, gravy is only at the table at Thanksgiving or special occasions.

The basic elements to remember are pan drippings or meat stock, fat, flour, and herbs. First measure your pan drippings; on average you need about a cup. You'll always need equal parts flour and butter.

Transfer chicken drippings from roasting pan to small skillet, on medium-low heat. (Another option is to remove whole chicken and place roasting pan on medium-low heat. You'll need to skim off the grease from the drippings. Too much fat will create an oily gravy.)

Pour in ¼ cup of stock to release chicken bits in bottom of the pan, using a spoon.

Place butter in pan, let melt.

Sprinkle in 2 tablespoons of flour. With a fork, mix well (this will prevent lumps). Then add another tablespoon, mix with fork.

At this point, the gravy will tighten a bit but slide off a spoon. If too thick, add a teaspoon or so of stock and no more flour. If still loose, add another tablespoon of flour, mix well.

Sprinkle in herbs, salt, and pepper. There should be no lumps in gravy. If so, mix again with fork.

Your gravy should barely coat a spoon but not stick. If it sticks, add more stock.

If you still detect lumps, you'll need to use additional stock.

Serve warm.

Sautéed Soft-Shell Crab

The last meal I cooked up for my beloved Uncle Charles was soft-shell crabs. I zoomed all over Atlanta to find them. Fondly, I remember him asking, "Do I eat the shell and all?" Yes, chow down!

Feeds 3

6 soft-shell crabs, cleaned (about 8 pounds)

½ teaspoon coarse salt

1 teaspoon The Franks seasoning (see Fish and Seafood Fry, page 89)

3 tablespoons pecan oil

4 tablespoons compound butter (see Whole Roasted Bird, page 92)

Ask your fishmonger to clean the crabs. Rinse them and pat dry. Season the crabs with the salt and seasoning mix.

In a 12-inch skillet on medium-high heat, add the oil and butter. (If you don't have compound butter on hand, add 4 tablespoons butter, 2 finely chopped garlic gloves, and 1 teaspoon of finely chopped parsley in skillet.) Add the crabs, cooking for 3 minutes each side.

Serve immediately.

Lime Catfish with Sweet Potatoes and Macadamia Nuts

Fresh fish reminds me of Wilfong's, which is now a parking lot in Athens, Georgia. The place had wooden floors, and it smelled like the sea. I was so fascinated by all the tiny pebbles of ice and the glazed eyes of the creatures.

When choosing fish from skilled fishmongers, they'll ask if you want it gutted and cleaned. Say yes, and ask that they keep the head on. Also, any nut or nut oil will work fine in this recipe.

Feeds 2

1 small sweet potato, sliced (⅓ pound)
⅓ cup macadamia nuts, toasted and
   chopped
1 teaspoon coarse salt, divided
¼ teaspoon ground white pepper, more
   optional
2 tablespoons plus 1 teaspoon macadamia
   oil, divided
6 tablespoons fresh lime juice
   (about 3 limes)
1½ teaspoons honey
2 medium pieces catfish, filleted
   (about 1 pound)
¼ teaspoon red pepper flakes
2 tablespoons unsalted butter

Preheat the oven to 375°F.

Rinse and gently scrub the sweet potato with a vegetable brush. Using a mandoline, set to the thickest slice and process the sweet potato.

Place nuts in a 12-inch skillet, over medium heat. Shake skillet a bit to move nuts around. Toast for 10 minutes. Set aside.

In a roasting pan, place the cut sweet potato slices about a ½ inch apart. Add ¼ teaspoon of the salt, the white pepper, and drizzle 1 teaspoon of the macadamia oil. Roast for 15 minutes and set aside.

In a small mixing bowl, add 2 tablespoons of macadamia oil and lime juice. Whisk in honey; add ½ teaspoon salt and white pepper to taste. Put aside.

Rinse and pat dry fish (already cleaned, cut, and filleted). Season both sides with remaining ¼ teaspoon salt and red pepper flakes.

In a grill pan, melt butter on medium-high heat. Cook for about 4 minutes (on each side), turn with a fish spatula. To tell the doneness of fish, it should have a gentle flake and be opaque inside.

Pour the lime mixture over the fish and cook for an additional 4 minutes. Plate half the sweet potato on each plate. Place the fish and drippings on top. Sprinkle nuts on fish.

Salmon Patties

Until recently, I frowned upon canned protein because I didn't understand its value. But salmon, even from a can, is full of omega-3 fatty acids. And one can of salmon goes a long way.

Feeds 2–4

1 (14¾-ounce) can salmon

2 large eggs

½ cup bread crumbs

½ cup green onions (¼ pound)

3 tablespoons crème fraîche

1 tablespoon fresh parsley, chopped

1 teaspoon coarse salt

1 tablespoon lemon juice (about ½ lemon)

¼ teaspoon red pepper flakes

1½ cups sunflower oil

The canned salmon often has bones in it. Slowly pick out the salmon from the can, placing the chunks of fish in a large bowl.

Combine all other ingredients (besides oil) into the bowl. Stir well until combined.

In a 12-inch skillet on medium-high heat, heat the oil to 350°F, using an instant-read thermometer. Cook the patties 3 minutes on each side.

Whole Roasted Duck and Cherries

North Carolina has Cheerwine, but Athens, Georgia had Budwine, the original cherry soda. It was strong like a ginger beer with real cherry flavor. Budwine ceased production in the mid-1990s, but the memories live on.

Feeds 4–6

CHERRY SAUCE

Makes 2 cups

1 cup pitted, fresh, dark sweet cherries, chopped

12 ounces Cheerwine (or another cherry soda)

½ teaspoon coarse salt

Large pinch ground black pepper

⅓ cup chopped onions (about ½ large onion)

⅓ cup chopped fresh parsley

⅓ cup red wine

1 tablespoon lime juice (from ½ lime)

WHOLE ROASTED DUCK

1 whole duck (about 8 pounds)

1 tablespoon coarse salt

1 teaspoon ground black pepper

4 whole lemons (1 pound)

1 small bunch fresh thyme

The cherry sauce: In a heavy saucepan on medium heat, combine all cherry sauce ingredients. Let cook, uncovered, for 20 minutes.

The whole roasted duck: Rinse the duck and pat dry. Season with salt and pepper. Cover and refrigerate, at least 30 minutes.

Preheat the oven to 400°F. Prepare your pan by lining a rimmed baking sheet with aluminum foil. Place an ovenproof baking pan on top.

Remove the duck from refrigerator; stuff the lemons and fresh thyme into the cavity of the bird. Place the duck onto the baking sheet and bake for 40 minutes.

Take the pan out of the oven and flip the duck over. If the pan has a large amount of duck fat in the bottom, you can drain this off, reserving for future use.

Put the duck back into the oven for an additional 35 minutes. Internal temperature should be around 165°F; skin will be crispy.

Remove from oven, let rest, and place the duck on a platter. Serve with the cherry sauce.

Reserve duck fat and use like butter.

Chicken Stock

Never throw out the bone of a whole chicken. Make plans for stock instead.

Makes 5 cups

12 cups water

2 small chicken carcasses

2 cups onions, chopped rough (2 large onions)

4 stalks celery, chopped rough (about 1 pound)

4 carrots, chopped rough (about ½ pound)

4 garlic cloves, smashed

3 tablespoons fresh thyme

2 teaspoons whole black peppercorns

1 tablespoon coarse salt

2 dried or fresh bay leaves

Place all ingredients in 12-quart stockpot, over high heat. Cover with lid.

Bring all ingredients to a boil. Reduce to medium-low heat.

Simmer for 3 hours. Remove fat during cooking time by skimming the top, using a large spoon.

Let cool completely.

Strain. Discard bones and vegetables.

Place in freezer for several months or fridge for about 3 days.

Red and White Meat

Southern saying: "My lawdy, she is at every hog killin'."

No Memphis vs. St. Louis or North Carolina vs. South Carolina BBQ ramblings here. I only cook out three times per year because hauling my Weber Smokey Joe from Brooklyn's Fort Greene Park or Prospect Park is a task. Basically, I fix burgers and sausages on the grill and the rest is whipped up inside.

The majority of my Empire State charred-and-smoked memories are created with a stovetop grill pan and a constant eye on the bottom of the oven. Once, after slow roasting a pork shoulder while I slept, the fat dripped (I forgot to place a pan under the roasting sheet to catch accidents), and the smoke woke up my entire building at 3 a.m.—I learned my lesson.

Venison and Beef Burger

Visiting home after living in two different cities and being a vegetarian is tricky. My family is confused about my culinary likes. The surprise on their faces when I'm hunting down deer meat is amusing. Deer roam back home like bodega cats in Brooklyn— they are always around and sneak up on you. Venison is super lean, and so I add beef and fat to the mix.

Feeds 8

1 pound ground grass-fed beef
½ pound beef fat
1 pound ground venison (see note)
1½ teaspoons coarse salt
¼ teaspoon ground black pepper

Sprinkle cold meats with salt and pepper. Gingerly combine meat. Don't overmix.

Preheat a grill pan on high heat.

Form the patties; they should be 4 inches wide, ½ inch tall. Feel free to freeze any patties for a future meal.

Place burgers in pan and fry for about 5 minutes per side. You'll get a medium or medium-well burger (a little pink in the inside).

The outside of the patties should have a slight crisp and inside should be juicy and not dry.

Use your favorite potato roll or buns here.

Note: Be sure to call ahead or inquire with specialty food distributors about venison. Your overall meat-to-fat ratio should be around 70/30. If grinding all your meat at home (including beef or pork fat), don't forget to ask your butcher for the correct ratio. Remember that grass-fed beef tends to be leaner than corn-fed beef. A trained butcher will understand this lingo.

Dry Rub Pork Spare Ribs

NYC-style barbeque is a thing. I must admit, my adopted home has a handful of eating places that do 'cue well. However, my motto remains: Someone is doing it better at home. Get the best meat your money can buy and go for it!

Feeds 4–6

4 pounds pork spare ribs

4 tablespoons coarse salt, divided

1 tablespoon plus 2½ teaspoons black pepper, divided

1 cup dark brown sugar, packed

3 tablespoons liquid smoke

1½ teaspoons smoked paprika

1½ teaspoons red pepper flakes

1 teaspoon mustard powder

1 teaspoon ground cinnamon

1 teaspoon ground cumin

1 teaspoon onion powder

1 teaspoon garlic powder

1 tablespoon fresh thyme

1 tablespoon fresh parsley, chopped

½ teaspoon ground allspice

½ teaspoon chili powder

Rinse and pat the pork ribs dry. Season the ribs with 1 tablespoon of the salt and 1½ teaspoons of the black pepper.

Combine the remaining salt and pepper with all remaining ingredients. This is your dry rub.

Cover all the ribs, both sides, with the rub. Cover and refrigerate for at least 3 hours, or overnight.

Preheat the oven to 350°F.

Transfer ribs to a lipped baking sheet or jelly roll pan, lined with a cooling rack. For easy cleanup, place foil at bottom of sheet or pan. In addition, place a baking sheet on bottom rack to catch any drippings (this will prevent the oven from smoking).

Cook the ribs uncovered for 1½ hours. Cover with foil and cook an additional 45 minutes.

The internal temperature of the ribs should be around 180°F.

The ribs will have a deep brown color and the meat should easily come off the bone when done.

Beef Short Ribs

Heritage Foods USA was started in 2001 as a marketing arm of Slow Food USA. The founder, Patrick Martins, keeps me knowledgeable about meat and farmers, from grass to mouth. I'm excited that his warehouse in the Bushwick neighborhood of Brooklyn is stocked with products from Georgia-based White Oak Pastures.

Feeds 2–3

1½ pounds short ribs, bone in
1½ teaspoons granulated sugar
1½ teaspoons cocoa powder
¼ teaspoon chili powder
¼ teaspoon ground cinnamon
¼ teaspoon ground allspice
¼ teaspoon salt
¼ teaspoon ground black pepper
2 tablespoons olive oil
3 cups red wine
4 sprigs sage
4 sprigs thyme
2 carrots, chopped rough (⅓ pound)
2 turnips, chopped rough (½ pound)
2 cups onions, chopped rough
   (2 large onions)
2 potatoes, chopped rough (1 pound)

Rinse and pat the ribs dry. Season the ribs with sugar, cocoa, chili powder, cinnamon, allspice, salt, and pepper.

Cover and refrigerate for a minimum of 1 hour or overnight.

Preheat oven to 325°F.

Using a large Dutch oven on high heat, add olive oil to large Dutch oven. Sear the short ribs until brown, about 5 minutes on each side.

Add wine, sage, and thyme. Put in oven.

Cook for 3 hours. At 1½ hours, add carrots, turnips, onions, and potatoes. Cook for an additional 1½ hours.

The internal temperature should be around 180°F. The ribs should pull right off the bone.

Remove from oven and let rest or cool down before serving.

Bone-In Roast Pork Shoulder

Every table, and person, needs an anchor: a symbolic dish of stability. I learned that indirectly from my late cousins Tom and Bonnie Gartrell. Their home is where love overflowed. It's the place I first saw a pig roast and saw love in action. The abundance of memories influences my approach when catering to family and new friends.

Feeds 6

6 pounds pork shoulder (bone-in)

1 cup coarse salt

1 teaspoon red pepper flakes

1½ teaspoons ground black pepper

2 teaspoons ground cumin

½ teaspoon smoked paprika

½ teaspoon garlic powder

½ teaspoon onion powder

Rinse and pat shoulder dry. Season the pork with salt, red pepper flakes, black pepper, cumin, paprika, garlic powder, and onion powder.

Cover and refrigerate for a minimum of 1 hour or overnight.

Preheat oven to 250°F.

Transfer pork shoulder to a lipped baking sheet or jelly roll pan, lined with a cooling rack. For easy cleanup, place foil at bottom of sheet or pan. In addition, place a baking sheet on bottom rack to catch any drippings (this will prevent the oven from smoking).

Cook the shoulder uncovered for 5 hours. Cover with foil and cook an additional 2 hours. During the final 2 hours check the internal temperature a few times. The bone size affects the cooking time.

The internal temperature should be around 160°F. The pork meat should pull away easily from fat and bone.

Remove from oven. Let rest and cool before pulling the meat, minimum of 30 minutes.

Country Ham and Red Eye Gravy

I'll blame the Big Apple for my java addiction. Burning the midnight oil is preceded by a strong cup of coffee—black. Making extra for ice cubes or saving a bit for gravy can be a good idea. For sure, country ham and gravy is a throwback breakfast. Ask your butcher for the bone-in cut.

Feeds 2-4

2½ pounds ham steak (1 inch thick)
½ teaspoon ground black pepper, plus small pinch (optional)
2 tablespoons unsalted butter
½ cup brewed dark coffee
2 tablespoons flour
Small pinch salt (optional)

Rinse and pat dry the ham steak. Sprinkle with ½ teaspoon black pepper.

Heat a 12-inch skillet on medium-high heat. Add butter.

Place the ham steak in skillet, cook for 12 minutes on each side. The internal temperature should be around 140°F. Remove from pan and set aside on large plate.

Add dark coffee to ham drippings. Scrape bits from bottom of the pan with a wooden spoon.

Sprinkle in flour and use spoon to smooth out lumps. Cook on medium heat for 5–10 minutes.

Season to taste with more black pepper and salt, if using.

Liver and Smothered Onions

Looking for an iron-rich meal? Eat liver. It's best with loads of onions and garlic. This is an economical piece of meat that can feed a tribe.

Feeds 4–6

1 pound beef liver, sliced (about ¼ inch thick)

2½ teaspoons coarse salt, divided

3 teaspoons pepper, divided

1 cup flour

¼ cup sunflower oil

3 tablespoons unsalted butter

3 cups thinly sliced onions (4 medium onions)

¼ cup garlic, minced (about 4 cloves)

Season the liver with 1½ teaspoons of the salt and 1 teaspoon of the pepper.

Whisk together the flour, 1 teaspoon salt, and 1 teaspoon pepper. Dredge the liver in the seasoned flour.

In a 12-inch cast-iron skillet on high heat, add the oil and butter. Once the butter is melted, add the liver slices in two batches. Cook the liver for 3 minutes, flip and cook an additional 3 minutes. Remove from pan.

Turn the heat to medium, add all cooked liver back to the pan along with the onions and garlic. Cook it all together for an additional 6 minutes.

Don't overcook. The liver should be tender, not tough, when cutting.

Fennel and Sage Sausage Patties

After 10-plus years of zero red and white meat touching my lips, I had my first taste of meat at The Frying Pan, a seasonal restaurant and bar boat docked on Manhattan's Pier 66. This experience opened the floodgates of eating pork again. Double this batch and freeze for a future breakfast. I'll never go back to buying store-made breakfast sausages.

Makes 10

1¼ pounds boneless pork shoulder (see note)

1 tablespoon plus 1½ teaspoons dried fennel seeds

2 tablespoons fresh sage, rubbed

½ teaspoon ground sage

1 tablespoon fresh finely chopped parsley

2 teaspoons coarse salt

1 teaspoon black pepper

1 teaspoon red pepper flakes

½ teaspoon onion powder

Chop the pork into large cubes. Make sure that the meat stays very cold for the grinding process.

Using a mortar and pestle, roughly grind up the fennel seeds. (If you do not have a mortar and pestle, sandwich the fennel seeds in parchment paper and use a rolling pin to break up the seeds.)

Mix together the fennel with the remaining ingredients.

Using a ¼-cup measuring cup, form the patties. Heat a 12-inch skillet on medium heat, and fry the sausage for 5 minutes per side.

The outside of the patties should have a slight crisp and inside should be juicy and not dry.

Note: When shopping for your pork, ask your butcher to take out the bones from the shoulder, but make sure the shoulder still has some fat on it. If you don't have a meat grinder, feel free to ask your butcher for high-quality ground pork shoulder.

Leaf Lard

The white gold of the South is back in style. It is a super easy DIY task. Lard can get a bit pricey at specialty grocers and farmers' markets. I say try making it at home once.

Makes about 6 cups

1½ pounds lard

Preheat oven to 325°F.

Put lard in a 12-inch cast-iron skillet, place in oven, and cook for one hour. Remove any meat from the fat.

Use strainer and cheesecloth to remove small particles.

Cool and transfer lard, or fatback, to container. Use the same way as you would for other oils, fats, or butter.

Ginger and Pear Pork Chops

My four-story apartment building is located in Central Brooklyn. The largest concentration of individuals of Caribbean descent living outside of the Caribbean calls my neighborhood home. I can walk in any direction and find multiple forms of ginger. Use a spoon to remove the skin off fresh ginger. A ceramic ginger grater is helpful in reducing strings of fiber but is not a necessity.

Feeds 4

MARINADE

3 tablespoons olive oil
3 tablespoons lemon juice (about 1 lemon)
¼ teaspoon ground ginger
¼ teaspoon red pepper flakes
¼ teaspoon coarse salt
Small pinch ground black pepper

PEAR PORK CHOPS

4 center bone-in pork chops
    (about 4 pounds)
4 tablespoons unsalted butter
1½ cups chopped Bosc pears
    (about 2 pears)
1 tablespoon fresh ginger, grated
½ teaspoon coarse salt
¼ teaspoon ground black pepper

Mix together all ingredients for the marinade.

Pour over the pork chops and marinate for 1 hour minimum or up to 24 hours.

Preheat your broiler, highest temperature.

Place a grill pan on the stovetop on high heat and let the pan heat up.

Sear the pork chops for 5 minutes, flip, and cook for another 3 minutes on the opposite side. Add the butter, pears, ginger, salt, and pepper.

Cook for another two minutes on the stove. The chops should have grill marks on each side.

Place the pan into your broiler and cook for 10 minutes, temperature should be high.

The chops should reach an internal temperature of around 145°F. The chops will be a bit caramelized.

Pork Stock

This is my motto for indulging in swine: Everything in moderation and buy the best.

Makes 4½ cups

10 cups water

2 fresh ham hocks (1½–2 pounds)

3 whole leeks or 6 green leek tops, chopped rough (about 1 pound)

4 whole cloves garlic, smashed

1 dried or fresh bay leaf

1 tablespoon fresh thyme

1 tablespoon fresh parsley, chopped

½ teaspoon ground black pepper

Place all ingredients in 12-quart stockpot, over high heat. Cover with lid.

Bring all ingredients to a boil. Reduce to medium-low heat.

Simmer for 3 hours minimum. Remove fat during cooking time by skimming the top, using a large spoon.

Let cool completely.

Strain. Discard bones, meat, and vegetables.

Place in freezer for several months or fridge for about 3 days.

Fried Fatback

A versatile provision. Cut bacon-style strips and use instead of oil or to season a pot of beans. I've seen folks eat it as a side protein with vegetables or biscuits.

Also, you can cook down the entire slab and use it in the same manner as lard. Here are the steps for making a solid. Remember to rinse salt-cured fatback when using it in any way.

Makes about 6 cups

1½ pounds fatback

Preheat oven to 325°F.

In a 12-inch cast-iron skillet, place fatback on its belly, put skillet in oven, and cook for 1 hour. Remove any meat from the fat.

Use strainer and cheesecloth to remove small particles.

Cool and transfer fatback to container. Use the same way as lard or in place of butter.

Bread and Biscuits

Southern saying: "Six of one, half-dozen of the other."

Thank you for the food we are about to receive. Bless the hands that prepared it and the folks sitting around the table.

I acknowledge the endless church functions that shaped my palate and the yearly repast of my family's first-cousin gathering. I'm beholden to you for the privilege to explore life outside the South and to break bread with a "new family."

Father, I ask for forgiveness for the person who adds more than a pinch of sugar to their cornbread (they don't know any better). Furthermore, I request the death of box corn muffin mixes, can biscuits, and low-fat buttermilk. Now, let's eat!

Amen.

Cornbread

The cast-iron wars, also known as the bickering among my two aunts and mother. Three sixty-year-old skillets are treasures in my immediate family. You can't borrow them because my Aunt Joann spazzes out. Seasoned pans make a woman go crazy!

Feeds 6

6 tablespoons unsalted butter
1¾ cups fine cornmeal
1 teaspoon coarse salt
1 teaspoon baking powder
1½ cups buttermilk
2 large eggs, lightly beaten
⅓ cup pork crackling pieces (optional)

Preheat oven to 400°F.

Add the butter to an 8-inch cast-iron skillet and place in oven for about 10 minutes.

Combine cornmeal, salt, and baking powder in a large bowl. Whisk together well. Stir in buttermilk and eggs.

Remove pan from oven. Carefully, pour hot butter into the cornmeal mixture. Whisk together well. If using cracklings, stir them in now.

Pour the batter into the hot skillet. This ensures a deep brown crust.

Place in middle rack and bake for 45 minutes.

Serve warm.

Note: My mother likes to add crackling or crispy pork bits to the batter.

Hot Water Cornbread

My husband calls this bread barefoot cornbread. I suspect this method of bread was put into practice when there were bare ingredients and zero dairy on hand. I use regular cornmeal, not self-rising (which contains the leavening agent).

Feeds 6

1¼ cups boiling water
¾ cup sunflower oil
1½ cups fine cornmeal
1 teaspoon coarse salt
1 teaspoon baking powder
¼ teaspoon granulated sugar

Boil a kettle of water.

Place oil into a large skillet over high heat. Insert an instant-read thermometer in oil. When the temperature reaches 225°F, the corn mixture is ready for the skillet.

Combine cornmeal, salt, baking powder, and sugar. Mix well. Measure out 1¼ cups of the boiling water and pour into the cornmeal mixture. You should be ready to fry; don't let the batter set.

Carefully drop cornmeal mix in oil, around 3 tablespoons for each piece of bread. Work in batches. Cook for about 3 minutes on each side or until golden brown. Remember to let the oil reach the 225°F mark before dropping more mix and don't crowd the pan.

Transfer to jelly roll pan with cooling rack on top. Sprinkle with a pinch of salt.

Buttermilk Biscuits

When I think of biscuits from my childhood, my thoughts go directly to the now-closed Katherine's Kitchen on Atlanta Highway in Athens, Georgia. It is currently the location of a modern drive-thru. I remember a few family members working at Katherine's and stopping by for a country ham biscuit. When making this biscuit, remember to make haste and work quickly, and use cold dairy.

Makes 10

2½ cups all-purpose flour, plus 2 teaspoons to roll out dough

2 teaspoons baking powder

1 teaspoon baking soda

½ teaspoon coarse salt

½ cup unsalted cold butter (1 stick), plus 1 teaspoon to coat pan

1 cup buttermilk, plus 2 tablespoons for brushing on biscuits

Preheat the oven to 400°F.

Combine 2½ cups flour, baking powder, baking soda, and salt in a large bowl. Whisk together well.

Quickly cut the ½ cup cold butter into cubes. Incorporate the butter into the flour mixture with a pastry cutter. Typically, I put my cutter in the freezer before starting the biscuit-making process. It's okay to use your fingertips to incorporate butter, but your hand should be as cool as possible. Cut until the ingredients are pea-sized.

Make a well in the center of the bowl.

Add ½ cup of the buttermilk to the well.

Using your hands, gently incorporate the buttermilk into the biscuits. Add an additional ½ cup buttermilk and continue to gently mix together.

Sprinkle a flat surface with 2 teaspoons flour.

Transfer batter to surface using a pastry scraper. Another tip: place pastry scraper and rolling pin in the freezer. The goal is to have visible pieces of butter.

Gently knead 1 or 2 turns with rolling pin. Roll out to 1-inch thickness.

Dip a 3-inch biscuit cutter into your package of all-purpose flour; this helps with a flawless cut. Press cutter into dough.

When finished cutting, take the uncut dough and gather into round disk. Sprinkle a little more flour to your surface if needed. Repeat the rolling out and cutting process. For any remaining dough, press with cutter and/or shape into 3-inch circles.

Grease the bottom of a 12 × 17-inch baking sheet with 1 teaspoon remaining butter. Place the biscuits into the pan. They should almost touch.

Brush the tops of the biscuits with the remaining buttermilk. Place in middle rack position.

Bake for 15 minutes.

Don't throw day-old biscuits away; instead, toast and process for bread crumbs. If stored in an airtight container, they will last for a few weeks. These bread crumbs can be used in the Rice and Spring Onion Cakes (see page 30) and Rutabaga and Potato Gratin (see page 50) recipes.

Another option is to slice off the biscuit bottom with a serrated knife. Place in the broiler for about a minute and top with No Mayo Pimento Cheese (see page 54).

Looking for stuff to put on your biscuit? Try leftover fried fatback, sage and fennel sausage, lemon curd, fried green tomatoes, or citrus curd.

Note: I use a ½-inch cutter for mini biscuits: the perfect size for a cheese board.

Not-So-Sweet Cinnamon Buns

Baking bread scares me, but I've mastered the science of feel. The best tip is to practice, practice, practice, and take photos of the dough during each rise. This visual will assist in future batches. Yeast Rolls (see page 129) and these cinnamon rolls use the same dough recipe. Making one almost means you must make the other—if you so choose.

Feeds 10

FROSTING

4 tablespoons butter, softened

4 tablespoons powdered sugar

4 tablespoons ricotta cheese

FILLING

½ cup plus 3 tablespoons unsalted butter, room temperature

1 cup brown sugar, packed

2½ tablespoons ground cinnamon

1 teaspoon vanilla paste

Small pinch allspice

The frosting: Mix butter, powdered sugar, and cheese in a small bowl. Combine well and set aside.

The filling: Combine room-temperature butter with brown sugar and mix well, using spoon or paddle attachment of stand mixer.

Add cinnamon, vanilla, and allspice. Don't overmix; the butter mixture should be spreadable but not melting. Set aside in a cool place or fridge.

The buns: Combine yeast, warm water, and 1 teaspoon sugar in large bowl to activate the yeast. Let sit for 10 minutes.

In a large bowl, combine the flour, ¼ cup sugar, and salt. Add the yeast mixture and mix together. Add egg and stir until combined. Add buttermilk and stir together again. You will have a shaggy-looking dough. Add the 2 tablespoons melted butter and knead together until you have a smooth dough.

continued

BUNS

2¼ teaspoons active dry yeast, or 1 packet

¼ cup warm water

¼ cup plus 1 teaspoon granulated sugar, divided

2¼ cups all-purpose flour

½ teaspoon coarse salt

1 large egg, lightly beaten

¼ cup buttermilk

2 tablespoons unsalted butter (melted), plus ½ teaspoon butter (unmelted) to coat pan

Let rise for 1 hour. Punch down and knead lightly.

Roll out dough to ½ inch thick.

Spread filling onto rolled-out dough in even layer.

Roll up dough. Cut into 10 even slices, using a serrated knife.

Spread remaining ½ teaspoon butter in the bottom of two 9-inch cake pans. The buns should almost touch in pans. Let rise for another hour.

Halfway through rise, preheat the oven to 375°F.

Bake rolls for 20 minutes on middle rack.

Let the cinnamon buns cool a bit, and then spread frosting on them.

Yeast Rolls

During the Great Migration (1900–1970), around 6 million African Americans left the South and journeyed, mostly, north. My great-aunt Bessie Goolsby was one of those people. Before she moved "up nawth," she solidified her name as the best roll maker in Athens-Clarke County. Affectionately called Bess Goo, she worked as a cook at Lyons Junior High School.

Feeds 12

- 4½ teaspoons active dry yeast, or 2 packets
- ½ cup warm water
- ¾ cup plus 2 teaspoons granulated sugar
- 4½ cups all-purpose flour
- 1½ teaspoons coarse salt
- 2 large eggs, lightly beaten
- ½ cup buttermilk
- 4 tablespoons unsalted butter (melted), plus ½ teaspoon butter (unmelted) to coat pan

Combine yeast, warm water, and 2 teaspoons sugar in large bowl to activate the yeast. Let sit for 10 minutes.

In a large bowl, combine the flour, ¾ cup sugar, and salt. Add the yeast mixture and mix together. Add the eggs and stir until combined. Add buttermilk and stir together again. You will have a shaggy-looking dough. Add the melted butter and knead together until you have a smooth dough.

Let rise for 1 hour. Punch down and knead lightly.

Roll out dough to about ½ inch thick. Cut dough into long strips, and cut each strip into about 3-inch pieces. Take a strip of dough and roll, creating a rustic ball. Form the rolls so that the tops are smooth and bottoms are flat. They will look like imperfect golf balls. Place in buttered cake pan so they are barely touching, 12 in a pan. Let rise for 1 hour, until doubled in size.

Halfway through the second rise, preheat the oven to 375°F. Bake rolls for 20 minutes, or until golden brown.

Hush Puppies

Brooklyn native Melissa Danielle says, "I didn't have hush puppies until I visited an African American farmers' conference in Tillery, North Carolina." Her grandparents are from the Carolinas, but no one in her family circle made them. I use an ice cream scoop or melon baller to drop them into the oil. When they are done, the corn balls float to the top—magical.

Feeds 6

4 cups peanut oil

1½ cups fine cornmeal

½ tablespoon baking powder

1 teaspoon baking soda

½ teaspoon cream of tartar

1 teaspoon coarse salt

¼ teaspoon ground black pepper

½ teaspoon granulated sugar

¼ teaspoon red pepper flakes

2 large eggs, beaten

¾ cup buttermilk

⅓ cup chopped onion (about ½ large onion)

2 tablespoons chopped fresh parsley

Using a Dutch oven, heat oil on a high heat to 350°F (use an instant-read thermometer). You'll need a shallow pot here, not a skillet.

Combine cornmeal, baking powder, baking soda, cream of tartar, salt, pepper, sugar, and red pepper. Mix well.

Add eggs and buttermilk. Stir in onions and parsley.

Drop batter into hot oil with an ice cream scoop. Be careful of splattering oil and work quickly.

Cook for 2 minutes, in batches. The hush puppies will float to the top of the oil.

They should be crispy all over the outside and tender inside.

Use a spider (wire skimmer) to remove from oil. Place on cooling rack with a jelly roll pan on the bottom, which will drain any excess oil.

Pecan Cornbread Dressing

Mrs. Edna Lewis is the grand dame of Southern cooking, revered by Southern foodies. This recipe is adapted from the cookbook she cowrote titled *The Gift of Southern Cooking*.

Feeds 6

1 pan Cornbread (see page 121 for recipe)

½ cup chopped pecans

4 tablespoons butter (½ stick), plus 1 tablespoon to coat pan

2 tablespoons pecan oil

1½ cups chopped onions (about 2 large onions)

1 cup chopped celery (about 3 stalks)

½ cup fresh fennel, diced (about 1 medium bulb)

2 garlic cloves, minced

1 teaspoon dried sage

1 teaspoon coarse salt

¼ teaspoon ground black pepper

2 teaspoons fresh sage, rubbed

1 tablespoon fresh thyme

¾ cup chicken stock, divided

2 large eggs, lightly beaten

½ teaspoon liquid smoke

Crumble cornbread into a large mixing bowl. Set aside. Coat 7 x 11-inch pan with 1 tablespoon butter. Set aside.

Preheat oven to 350°F.

Toss pecans in a 12-inch skillet, over medium heat. Toast for 10 minutes. Add to cornbread bowl.

Melt 4 tablespoons butter in a skillet on medium heat. Pour in pecan oil. Add onions, celery, fennel, garlic, and dried sage. Cook and stir until slightly soft, around 15 minutes. Add to cornbread bowl.

Add salt and pepper to cornbread bowl and stir in fresh sage and thyme. Combine well.

Drop in fresh sage and thyme. Combine well.

Add half of the chicken stock and eggs. Stir well.

Add remaining stock and the liquid smoke. The dressing should not be too wet or dry. It should not stick to the spoon or fall without a shake.

Pour in liquid smoke.

Coat a 7 × 11-inch pan with 1 tablespoon butter and transfer pecan cornbread dressing.

Spread dressing in prepared pan and bake for 40 minutes. Let cool a little and serve warm.

Banana and Nut Bread

My life without peanuts is like President Jimmy Carter hating on Plains, Georgia—it'll never happen. I despise eating a plain banana from a bunch, but mashing it with other ingredients converts me. This banana loaf is perfect when brown pieces of fruit are staring at you.

Makes 1 loaf

- ¼ cup unsalted peanuts
- 2 large eggs
- 3 tablespoons unsalted butter (melted), plus 1 teaspoon to coat pan
- ½ cup buttermilk
- ⅓ cup smooth peanut butter
- 2 ripe bananas, mashed (½ pound)
- ½ cup granulated sugar
- ½ cup brown sugar, packed
- 1 cup all-purpose flour, plus 1 teaspoon to coat pan
- ½ cup peanut flour
- ¾ teaspoon baking soda
- ½ teaspoon coarse salt
- ½ teaspoon ground cardamom
- ½ teaspoon ground cinnamon

Preheat oven to 350°F.

Toss peanuts in a 12-inch skillet, over medium heat. Shake skillet a bit to move nuts around. Toast for 5 minutes. Set aside.

In the bowl of your stand mixer, or mix together by hand, add the eggs, melted 3 tablespoons butter, buttermilk, peanut butter, and mashed bananas. Mix on medium-low for 1 minute to combine.

In a separate medium bowl, combine sugars, flours, baking soda, salt, cardamom, and cinnamon. Mix well.

With the mixer on medium-low, slowly add the dry mixture. Mix until the flour is incorporated. Stir in peanuts.

Spread the remaining 1 teaspoon butter in a loaf pan. Sprinkle and coat the 1 teaspoon flour in same pan.

Pour cake batter in pan.

Bake for 60 minutes. Place on cooling rack.

Rose Sugar Donuts

Donuts are a quintessential Big Apple treat. My love affair with them started at the now defunct A&A Bakery in Athens, Georgia. My mother would treat me to a plain yeast, glazed. And rose is the first flower I fell in love with. My aunt would cut a stem off the front yard bush and pin it to my Easter dress. Take your pick of the rose sugar or lemon glaze for the donut.

Feeds 12

ROSE SUGAR

1 cup sugar

⅓ cup dried rose petals or 1 cup fresh

DONUTS

4½ teaspoons active dry yeast

1 cup warm water

¾ cup plus 2 teaspoons granulated sugar, divided

4½ cups all-purpose flour

1½ teaspoons coarse salt

2 large eggs, lightly beaten

¾ cup buttermilk

4 tablespoons unsalted butter, melted

4 cups sunflower oil or peanut oil

The rose sugar: Making the rose sugar can be done by hand, food processor, or Vitamix.

Combine sugar and petals. Pound until roses are in super small pieces.

If using either of the other methods, combine and pulse the sugar and petals a few times but don't overprocess. You want pieces to mix with the sugar.

The donuts: Combine yeast, warm water, and 2 teaspoons sugar in large bowl to activate the yeast. Let sit for 10 minutes.

In a separate large bowl, combine the flour, ¾ cup sugar, and salt. Add the yeast mixture and mix together. Add the eggs and stir until combined. Add buttermilk and stir together again. You will have a shaggy-looking dough. Add the melted butter and knead together until you have a smooth dough.

Let rise for 1 hour. Punch down. Knead slightly for a few minutes. Roll out dough to about ½ inch thick.

Cut into donuts using a donut cutter or a 3- and 1-inch circular biscuit cutter. Let rise for 1 hour, until doubled in size.

Pour oil in Dutch oven and let oil reach 375°F (use an instant-read thermometer).

Drop donuts in, but do not overcrowd pot. Fry the donuts for about 30 seconds, and then flip them over. Use skewers to flip over donuts. Be sure to keep an eye on thermometer and adjust flame to keep the heat at 375°F.

Transfer hot donuts to a cooling rack–lined jelly roll pan.

Quickly roll each donut in rose sugar, while warm.

Note: Another option is to deeply cool the donuts, and then top with the lemon glaze from the Lemon Pound Cake recipe (see page 139).

Cakes and Pies

Southern saying: "Cold hands equal a warm heart."

At 5 years old, I remember placing my Delta Airlines wings on my navy blue wool coat and traveling solo to Washington, DC. Spending a summer with one of my great-aunts taught me one lesson—food is a ritual. You make certain cakes and pies for special people and important days. Christmas Eve's dinner at the Gartrell house always meant a red velvet cake slice for dessert and a counter loaded with whole layer cakes with bows on top.

Lemon Pound Cake

My maternal grandparents had thirteen children. I have fond memories of most of them. I remember my great-aunt Lois ironing linen for the church's communion table and baking her famous pound cake. She was a little lady with a quiet spirit. This recipe embodies the stillness of women who were unselfish givers inside and outside the home.

Feeds 14

LEMON GLAZE

¼ cup fresh lemon juice (about 1½ lemons)

2 cups powdered sugar

1 tablespoon plus 1½ teaspoons lemon zest (about 2 lemons)

POUND CAKE

1 cup unsalted butter (3 sticks), plus 1 tablespoon to coat pan

1 cup cream cheese (8-ounce package)

3 cups granulated sugar

6 large eggs

3 cups all-purpose sifted flour, plus 4 tablespoons to coat pan

1 teaspoon vanilla paste or extract (see note)

¼ cup lemon juice (about 1½ lemons)

The lemon glaze: Combine lemon juice, sugar, and lemon zest using a whisk. Set aside.

Preheat oven to 325°F. Butter and flour a 9-inch Bundt pan (flour well and shake out excess). Set aside.

Using a stand or hand mixer, cream 1 cup butter and cream cheese. Gradually add sugar and beat until fluffy. Slowly add eggs, one at a time. In stages, incorporate sifted 3 cups flour but do not overbeat.

Add vanilla and lemon juice into mixture (the batter will be thick). Transfer into pan. Cooking time is around 1 hour and 30 minutes. Use the toothpick method to test doneness (place toothpick in center of the cake; if no batter sticks, it means the cake is done).

Transfer to cooling rack and let cool in cake pan. Loosen cake by running a butter knife around edges of the pan. Carefully turn out cake on a cake stand or plate.

Pour glaze over cake and let set for an hour.

Note: Vanilla paste has a thicker consistency, with specks of vanilla and a deeper flavor.

Fried Quince Pies

Nothing says the American South better than a fried pie. A flaky dough, the right amount of just-sweet fruit, and a greasy brown bag or envelope-like bag with the pie peeking out. I use quince, though I didn't ever taste it until moving to the Northeast. Remember, never eat quince raw; it must be cooked first. If you can't find quince, use pears.

Feeds 12

CRUST
1 cup lard
4 cups all-purpose flour
1 cup ice water
1 teaspoon coarse salt
½ cup buttermilk

QUINCE PIES
4 cups sliced quince (about 2⅔ pounds)
2 tablespoons plus 1 teaspoon light brown
    sugar, packed
1 tablespoon unsalted butter
½ teaspoon ground cinnamon
¼ teaspoon ground cardamom
¼ teaspoon ground ginger
¼ teaspoon ground nutmeg
¼ teaspoon vanilla paste
¼ teaspoon coarse salt
½ tablespoon all-purpose flour
1½ cups lard
1 cup granulated sugar

The crust: Using a pastry cutter or two forks, integrate 1 cup lard into the flour. You're looking for small, pea-sized crumbs. Add the water, salt, and buttermilk.

Roll the dough out until ½ inch thick. Cut out large 4-inch circles (see note). Place in fridge until ready to add quince.

The quince pies: Peel and core the quince. Chop into coarse medium-sized pieces.

In a 12-inch skillet on medium heat, combine the quince, light brown sugar, butter, cinnamon, cardamom, ginger, nutmeg, vanilla, and salt. Cover and bring to a bubble. Lower the heat and let simmer for about 15 minutes. Once softened, remove from heat and stir in the flour. Let cool a bit.

In the center of each pie circle, add one tablespoon of quince mixture. Fold the dough over and use a fork to press the edges closed.

In a large cast-iron skillet, add the 1½ cups lard. Once the oil has reached 350°F, using an instant-read thermometer, add half the pies. Fry for 3—4

minutes, then flip and fry for an additional 3–4 minutes. Repeat with the second half of pies.

Remove and place on cooling rack. Roll each pie in shallow bowl of granulated sugar.

Note: Your classic metal sifter is a great tool for cutting the pastry dough circles.

Red Velvet Cheesecake

What I know for sure is that my Aunt Jean can make a perfect red velvet cake. I'll say that it's the one thing that she never burned or fell asleep on. I knew it was baking time when she pulled down her yellow recipe box. She would always say this is "one expensive cake" and remind me that the liquid fat gave the batter its moisture. The key to this dessert is using the finest ingredients and taking care. The cheesecake layer is my homage to classic New York City.

Feeds 12

RED VELVET CAKE

½ cup granulated sugar

¾ cup all-purpose flour, plus 1 tablespoon to coat pan

1½ teaspoons cocoa powder

1 teaspoon baking powder

Small pinch coarse salt

1 large egg

¼ cup sunflower oil

¼ cup coconut oil

⅓ cup buttermilk

¼ teaspoon vanilla paste

¼ teaspoon red gel food coloring

1 teaspoon butter to coat pan

CHEESECAKE

3 cups cream cheese (24 ounces)

1 cup granulated sugar

¾ cup heavy cream

¼ teaspoon coarse salt

3 large eggs, lightly beaten

1½ teaspoons lemon juice (about ½ lemon)

The red velvet cake: Preheat oven to 325°F. In a large bowl, combine all dry ingredients. Whisk together to combine.

In the bowl of your stand mixer, or a large bowl, add the egg and oils. Mix on medium-low for 1 minute to combine.

Add the buttermilk, vanilla, and red gel. Mix on medium-low for 1 minute to combine.

With the mixer on medium-low, slowly add the dry mixture. Mix until the flour is just incorporated.

Butter and flour (shake off excess) a 10-inch spring-form pan. Pour the batter into the pan and bake for 35 minutes. Let cake completely cool.

The cheesecake: In the bowl of your stand mixer, combine the cream cheese, sugar, heavy cream, and salt. Beat together until thoroughly mixed. Add the eggs, beat together. Stir in the lemon juice.

continued

CREAM CHEESE FROSTING

½ cup cream cheese (4 ounces)

4 tablespoons unsalted butter, softened

½ cup powdered sugar

¼ teaspoon vanilla paste

½ cup chopped pecans

Pour on top of the cooled red velvet cake in the springform pan. Bake at 325°F for 45 minutes.

Remove from the oven and cool on a rack. The cheesecake will look slightly golden. Let cool completely.

The cream cheese frosting: In the bowl of your stand mixer or a large bowl, add the cream cheese and softened butter. Mix on medium speed until combined.

Slowly add the powdered sugar, a few spoonfuls at a time. Pour in vanilla paste.

Spread the frosting on the cooled cheesecake and sprinkle the pecans evenly on top of the frosting. Store in the fridge.

Note: My go-to flours are King Arthur All-Purpose and White Lily. I stuff my suitcase with this Southern staple when returning from trips down south. Everyone knows that Dixie cooks love using White Lily Flour to create desserts. Once milled in Knoxville, Tennessee, and later bought by The J. M. Smucker Company in 2006.

A few years back, I moderated a Red Velvet Cake Debate (hosted by Nichelle Stephens co-founder of Cupcakes Take the Cake) where the banter centered on technique. The most important and final question posed was if the red velvet sweet treat was just a fad. But, for sure, red velvet is part of the long-lived traditions of home bakers and pastry professionals.

Citrus Meringue Pie

After going over every recipe in this cookbook, my mama insisted on adding a lemon meringue pie. For the record, she always buys the popular frozen store-bought version, but I suspect she'll make this one now. I didn't have enough lemon on hand, and decided to use oranges and a lime. Each December I order a few bushels of citrus from a small Odessa, Florida grower named Cee Bee's Citrus. Almost any citrus combination will work here.

Feeds 8

PIE CRUST

1 (9-inch) Butter Pie Crust
   (see recipe, page 156)

MERINGUE

4 large egg whites
Small pinch cream of tartar
2 tablespoons granulated sugar

LEMON CURD

4 large egg yolks
4 large eggs
2 cups granulated sugar
1⅓ cups fresh mixed citrus juice (about 1
   lime, 2 oranges, and 3 lemons)
1½ cups unsalted butter, softened (3 sticks)
2 teaspoons grated lemon zest
   (about 1 lemon)

The pie crust: Parbake pie crust at 375°F for 30 minutes. Crust should be a light golden color. Rest pie on rack and let cool completely.

The meringue: Combine egg whites and cream of tartar, using the whisk attachment on a stand mixer or a hand mixer. Mix on medium-high speed until the whites have reached a soft peak (the peaks will bend). Slowly sprinkle in sugar.

Whisk mixture until stiff peaks form (the peaks will not bend and the mixture looks glossy).

The lemon curd: In a mixing bowl, whisk egg yolks, eggs, sugar, and citrus juice. Add butter, cut into pats in bowl. Place mixture in a heavy saucepan over low to medium heat.

Whisk and watch for about 15 minutes; the curd is ready when thick. Add lemon zest.

Pour curd into parbaked pie crust. Top or pipe with meringue. Place in oven for around 10 minutes or until you see a hint of gold on the meringue.

Note: Lemon curd can keep for several weeks in the refrigerator.

Peanut Butter Roll Cake

As I traveled to my hometown for inspiration and to collect stories about my maternal family, I was reminded of my great-aunt Mattie Willis's peanut butter cake. My cousin Shirley Ann gloated that Mat always made this cake for her birthdays. I decided to try my hand at keeping her tradition alive. The roll cake is a sponge cake filled with frosting. Be patient when rolling the warm dough, and don't be afraid to cover the cracked sponge with extra frosting. For the frosting, very simple—use top-shelf peanut butter and real butter.

Feeds 8–10

PEANUT BUTTER SWISS MERINGUE BUTTERCREAM

5 large egg whites

¾ cup granulated sugar

¼ teaspoon coarse salt

2 cups unsalted softened butter, cut into 2-inch chunks (4 sticks)

1 teaspoon vanilla paste

1 cup smooth peanut butter, divided

CAKE

⅓ cup peanuts, chopped

2 cups all-purpose flour, plus 1 tablespoon to coat pan

2 teaspoons baking powder

1 teaspoon coarse salt

6 large eggs, separated

½ cup unsalted butter (1 stick), plus 1 tablespoon to coat pan

The peanut butter Swiss meringue buttercream: Set up a double boiler with simmering water on medium-low heat.

Add the egg whites, sugar, and salt to the bowl. Stand close by and stir regularly. The egg whites should not cook. The mixture is ready after about 5 minutes. Feel free to use a candy thermometer. If so, the temperature should reach 145°F.

Remove the bowl from the stove. Using the stand mixer or hand mixer with the whisk attachment, mix until the volume of the meringue has doubled. The bowl should be completely cool to the touch—if it is not, continue mixing until the bowl is cool.

Turn the mixer to medium-low and begin adding the butter. Add one chunk at a time, mixing for a few seconds between chunks. Once all butter has been added to the mixture, turn off the mixer and scrape down the sides of the bowl.

1½ cups granulated sugar

½ cup sour cream

¼ cup smooth peanut butter

½ teaspoon vanilla paste

Add the vanilla paste and ½ cup of the peanut butter. Mix for a minute. Taste the buttercream and add more peanut butter, if desired.

The cake: Preheat oven to 325°F.

Toss nuts in a 12-inch skillet, over medium heat. Shake skillet a bit to move nuts around. Toast for 5 minutes. Set aside.

Line a 17½ × 12-inch jelly roll pan with parchment paper. Butter and flour pan and set aside.

Combine flour, baking powder, and salt in a large mixing bowl. Set aside.

Crack and separate eggs. Set aside 4 yolks (use the remaining two for another dish) and all 6 egg whites. Place egg whites in a small bowl and hand whisk whites until they reach soft peaks. Set aside.

Using a stand or hand mixer, cream butter and sugar. Beat until fluffy. Slowly add egg yolks only, one at a time. Next, mix in sour cream, peanut butter, and vanilla.

In stages, incorporate flour mixture, but do not overbeat.

Fold soft-peak egg whites into batter.

Transfer batter to pan. Spread the batter evenly into the pan using an offset spatula.

Cooking time is about 25 minutes. Overbaking will prohibit a near-perfect roll, so use the toothpick method to test doneness (place toothpick in center of the cake; if no batter sticks, it means the cake is done). The cake should have a light color appearance and not browned.

Transfer to cooling rack and let cool for a few minutes. Loosen cake by running a butter knife around edges of the pan.

continued

Carefully turn out warm cake with parchment still on the bottom to a clean kitchen towel. Remove the parchment paper.

Start from the long edge; slowly roll warm cake with the kitchen towel as your anchor. Keep rolled with towel covering for around 5 minutes or so.

Unroll, carefully, and transfer back to pan. Let cool completely.

At this point, set aside your serving plate for the roll cake.

To assemble: With the cake still on the pan, spread half the buttercream frosting, starting in the middle of cake. Keep a 1½-inch border free of buttercream.

Next, roll for the final time. The cake might crack a bit but that is fine. Transfer to serving plate.

Spread the remaining buttercream on the cake. If you have cracks in the cake, be sure to cover with ample buttercream.

Sprinkle with chopped peanuts.

Pineapple-Black Walnut Upside Down Cake

I'm in love with nuts and enjoy the act of cracking them open. However, black walnuts are a beast. The boyfriend of my food friend and native New Yorker Jackie Gordon has a black walnut tree in his yard. A few years back she invited me over to process a few buckets. Growing up, I saw folks crack them up with a hammer, but in New York we used a cracker that sat on the floor. We pressed down with all our weight to open the shell. It's rewarding work but not for the faint of heart. I suggest buying Hammons Black Walnuts (a family-owned company). They are easily found in supermarkets nationwide.

Feeds 12

BLACK WALNUT SAUCE

2 tablespoons unsalted butter

¾ cup dark brown sugar, packed

¼ teaspoon ground ginger

¼ cup chopped black walnuts

4 shakes black walnut bitters (optional)

CAKE

½ whole fresh pineapple (about 1 pound)
  or 5 slices canned pineapple

2 large eggs

6 tablespoons unsalted butter, plus 1
  teaspoon to coat pan

½ cup buttermilk

½ cup whole milk

1 cup granulated sugar

1½ cups all-purpose flour, plus 1 teaspoon
  to coat pan

The black walnut sauce: Combine butter, sugar, ginger, and walnuts in small skillet, over medium-low heat. Mix well, until it reaches a deeper brown color, around 5 minutes. Shake in bitters, if using.

The cake: Preheat oven to 350°F.

Cut outer shell and remove eyes of one whole pineapple. Cut 5 slices, around ¼ inch thick, and set aside the rest. If using canned fruit, pat dry juice/liquid before placing in the pan.

Using an apple corer or paring knife, remove the core and discard. Set aside slices.

In the bowl of your stand mixer or hand mixer, add the eggs, 6 tablespoons butter, buttermilk, and milk. Mix on medium-low for 1 minute to combine.

continued

2 teaspoons baking powder

½ teaspoon coarse salt

¼ teaspoon ground cinnamon

½ teaspoon vanilla paste

Combine sugar, 1½ cups flour, baking powder, salt, and cinnamon. Mix well.

With the mixer on medium-low, slowly add the dry mixture. Mix until the flour is just incorporated. Add vanilla paste. Don't overmix.

Spread the remaining 1 teaspoon butter in a spring-form pan. Sprinkle and coat the 1 teaspoon flour in same pan.

Place one pineapple ring in the middle of the pan. Cut others in half and arrange around the edge of pan.

Spoon walnut sauce evenly over pineapples.

Next, pour cake batter in pan.

Bake for 60 minutes. Place on cooling rack.

Transfer cake to plate or stand with pineapple side up.

Savory Sweet Potato Pie

Yams are not the same as sweet potatoes. Just like Moleskines are not regular notebooks. My local corner market has many varieties of yams. All are hairy, large, and fibrous. Very different from Jewel, my favorite sweet potato variety. Garnets are an option and approved for this savory pie.

Feeds 6

3 large sweet potatoes (about 3 cups)
1 (9-inch) Butter Pie Crust (see recipe, page 156)
4 tablespoons butter
½ cup shredded manchego cheese (about ¼ pound)
¼ cup crumbled blue cheese (about 1 ounce)
3 large eggs, beaten
¼ teaspoon red pepper flakes
¾ teaspoon fresh sage
¼ teaspoon coarse salt
¼ ground black pepper
Small pinch ground nutmeg
¼ cup chopped spring onions (about 2 onions)

Preheat the oven to 375°F.

Using a vegetable brush, rinse and scrub grit off potatoes.

Using a baking sheet with parchment paper, roast potatoes for 45 minutes to 1 hour. They should be soft to the touch.

While potatoes are baking, roll out prepared butter pie crust dough into a tart pan and parbake for 8–12 minutes. Remove and convert to cooling rack.

Remove potatoes from oven and reduce temperature to 350°F, let cool a bit, and remove skins.

Add potatoes, butter, cheeses, eggs, spices, and onion into a large bowl. Stir mixture until smooth and combined.

Fill the pie crust with filling. Bake for 40 minutes.

Let cool for 15 minutes and serve.

Buttermilk Pie

Cats and dogs were falling out of the sky the day I made two pies for Culinary Historians of New York. The group was hosting a book event for Andrew Smith's *Starving the South* book, and I waited until the day of the event to purchase my baking supplies—finding high-quality buttermilk in my neighborhood can be like finding a needle in a haystack. The rain wreaked havoc on my pie crusts and threw me behind schedule. Luckily, I recovered by letting the silky filling set in the walk-in fridge where the festivities were being held. The famed food historian Anne Mendelson gave me two thumbs up.

Feeds 8

1 (9-inch) Butter Pie Crust (see recipe, page 156)

1 cup granulated sugar

3 tablespoons fine cornmeal

½ teaspoon coarse salt

½ teaspoon ground cardamom

½ teaspoon ground nutmeg

4 tablespoons unsalted butter

3 large egg yolks

1 cup sour cream

2 cups buttermilk

½ tablespoon vanilla paste

Preheat oven to 375°F.

Place prepared butter pie crust in oven and parbake for 8–12 minutes. Remove and convert to cooling rack.

In a large mixing bowl, whisk together sugar, cornmeal, salt, cardamom, and nutmeg. Then add butter, yolks, sour cream, buttermilk, and vanilla paste.

Pour into slightly cool parbaked shell and bake for 45 minutes. The center should be slightly jiggly when ready.

Convert to wire rack and let cool. Let set in refrigerator. Serve chilled.

Butter Pie Crust

For the best pie crust, I place the butter and pastry blender in the freezer while mixing the flour and salt. Cold ingredients and utensils help achieve a tender crust.

The recipe for Butter Pie Crust is used for several pies in this book. It is necessary to parbake the crust for most of these recipes. See specific recipes for parbaking times.

Makes 1 (9-inch) crust

1½ cups all-purpose flour, plus extra for rolling out dough
½ teaspoon coarse salt
1 teaspoon granulated sugar
½ cup unsalted butter, cold (1 stick)
¼ cup ice water, divided

Preheat the oven to 375°F.

In a large mixing bowl, combine flour, salt, and sugar. Using a pastry blender, cut the butter into the flour.

When the mixture resembles sand with lumps, sprinkle half the ice water on top and bring the mass of dough together. The water should only bring the dough together; the shape should be an imperfect ball. If needed, add more water if too loose.

Scoop dough onto parchment paper and press into a ball. Wrap tightly and place in the fridge for an hour. Chilling the dough is a must.

Lightly flour a surface. Using a rolling pin, roll out dough into a 10-inch circle (using a ruler for precision). Quickly transfer to a 9-inch pie pan. Gently press the dough into the pan, cut dough that hangs over the pan, and crimp the edges.

Reduce oven to 325°F.

Parbaking: Line the crust with parchment paper and place ceramic pie weights (or dried beans) on top. Place in oven and let the shell bake for time listed in recipe. Remove and convert to cooling rack.

Note: If your pie edge starts to brown too quickly, place strips of foil over the crust edges.

Hummingbird Cake

I love me some Nancie McDermott. She has authored 10 cookbooks and lives in North Carolina. Her spirit, support, and counsel are inspiration for a new generation of cookbook authors. It's an honor to receive this stunner from her. She describes it as such:

With an abundance of fruity goodness from pineapple and bananas, and a pleasing crunch of pecans in both the cake and the icing, this cake wins the hearts of almost everyone who tastes it. Southern Living magazine made it famous as a reader's recipe, published in the 1970s, back when carrot cake was transitioning from "new" to "classic." Made with vegetable oil rather than butter, it's simple to stir together. You don't even need a mixer for this one, and the contrast of fruity sweetness and tangy cream cheese frosting still makes people swoon. Hummingbird cake is over thirty years old now—we know its age, but what about that charming name? Is it so sweet that hummingbirds crave it? Is it so delicious, it makes people hum? Nobody knows, but everybody knows it's one marvelous, memorable, makeable Southern dessert.

Feeds 8

CAKE

Butter to coat pans

3 cups flour

2 cups granulated sugar

1 teaspoon cinnamon

1 teaspoon baking soda

½ teaspoon coarse salt

3 large eggs, beaten well

¾ cup vegetable oil

1 teaspoon pure vanilla extract

1 cup (one 8-ounce can) crushed pineapple, including liquid

The cake: Preheat the oven to 350°F. Generously butter two 9-inch round cake pans. Line each pan with a circle of waxed paper or parchment paper, buttering the paper as well after placing in the bottom of the cake pan. In a large mixing bowl, combine the flour, sugar, cinnamon, baking soda, and salt. Use a fork or a whisk to stir them together well.

Add the beaten eggs, oil, vanilla, crushed pineapple with its juice, mashed bananas, and pecans to the flour mixture in the large bowl. Use a large spoon or a spatula to mix everything together, stirring gently. Stir just enough to mix everything together evenly into a thick, rich batter.

3 ripe bananas (about 2 cups mashed
   bananas)
1 cup chopped pecans

CREAM CHEESE ICING WITH PECANS
1 cup cream cheese (one 8-ounce package)
¼ cup softened butter (4 tablespoons)
3½ cups powdered sugar (one 1-pound
   box)
1 teaspoon pure vanilla extract
¾ cup finely chopped pecans

Divide the batter evenly between the two cake pans, and bake the layers for 20 to 25 minutes, until the layers are nicely browned and just pulling away from the sides of the pans.

Place the cake layers on a wire rack or on folded kitchen towels and let them cool for 15 to 20 minutes. Then gently turn the cakes out onto plates and set them top side up to cool completely.

The frosting: Combine the cream cheese and the butter in a large bowl. Using a mixer, beat at low speed to combine them well. Beat on high speed until the mixture is fluffy and creamy.

Add the powdered sugar and the vanilla, and continue beating, stopping to scrape down the sides now and then. Beat until you have a rich, creamy, smooth, and spreadable frosting. Using a large spoon or a spatula, stir in the pecans and mix them in evenly.

To finish the cake, place one layer topside down on a large cake plate or cake stand. Spread frosting to cover the bottom well. Place the second layer on the frosted layer, topside up. Press very gently to bring the layers together.

Frost the sides, and then the top, spreading to cover the cake completely. Even out the frosting so you have a wonderful thick frosting all over the cake. Serve at room temperature.

Lemon Coconut Stack Cake

The guy behind The Way We Ate blog asked me to develop a recipe centered on Hattie McDaniel's 1940 Oscar win. My first assumption was that the first African American to win an Academy Award was a child of the South, but then I learned that, in fact, she called Denver, Colorado home and was born in Kansas. I wanted to express the essence of the *Gone with the Wind* star and decided on a knockout six-tier tribute. The classic texture of shredded coconut bothers me and prompted me to think about the many culinary uses of the coconut (hence, coconut chips instead of shredded coconut). This beauty is dedicated Mrs. McDaniel's grand Californian lifestyle and love for floral.

Feeds 18

FROSTING

2 cups mascarpone cheese (16 ounces)

2 cups powdered sugar

¼ teaspoon vanilla paste

½ cup coconut chips, unsweetened

LEMON CURD

4 large egg yolks

1 cup granulated sugar

½ cup fresh lemon juice (about 3 lemons)

½ cup unsalted butter (1 stick), cut into pats

2 teaspoons lemon zest (about 1 lemon)

Small pinch coarse salt

Fresh gardenia buds (garnish)

Preheat oven to 325°F. Butter and flour three 9-inch cake pans.

The frosting: Using a stand or hand mixer, combine cheese, sugar, vanilla paste, and coconut chips. Cover and place in the fridge.

The curd: In a mixing bowl, whisk egg yolks, sugar, and lemon juice. Add butter. Place mixture in a saucepan over low to medium heat.

Whisk and watch for about 15 minutes; the curd is ready when thick. Add lemon zest and salt. When cool, store in a container and place in the fridge.

For cake: Using a stand or hand mixer, cream butter and cream cheese. Gradually add sugar and beat until fluffy. Slowly add eggs, one at a time. Put coconut milk in the batter. In stages, incorporate sifted flour in, but do not overbeat. Pour vanilla into

CAKE

2¼ cups unsalted butter (4¼ sticks), plus 1
  tablespoon to coat pans
4½ cups all-purpose sifted flour, plus 4
  tablespoons to coat pans
1½ cups cream cheese (12 ounces)
4½ cups granulated sugar
9 large eggs
¼ cup coconut milk unsweetened
½ teaspoon vanilla paste

mixture (the batter will be thick). Transfer equally into three cake pans. Baking time is around 1 hour. Insert a toothpick to test doneness; if it comes out clean, it is done. Let cool in pan and then convert to cooling rack.

Begin to assemble the cake by cutting each layer in half with a serrated knife, careful to only do one continuous cut while halving. Line edge but don't cover the entire cake pedestal with parchment paper, this prevents icing from overflow. Lay the first half layer down and spoon on lemon curd. Stack the next layer and spread mascarpone icing. Repeat stacking and layering using curd, then icing. Be generous with the icing on the top of final layer and add a circle of curd in the center.

Dress the sides of the stack cake with an abundance of fresh gardenias.

Strawberry and Mulberry Shortcake

My first foraging experience—over 25 years ago—put me on a hunt for mulberries. We called it "shaking berry bushes." Fast forward to today: I now enlist my husband in my mission to map tree locations and gathering berries. Mulberries resemble blackberries but are smaller and quite tart. Typically, you don't find mulberries commercially, so it's okay to use blackberries or black raspberries here.

Feeds 10

BERRY MIXTURE

1 pound strawberries, whole (about 4 cups)

½ pound mulberries (about 2 cups)

½ teaspoon balsamic vinegar

1 tablespoon brown sugar

Small pinch coarse salt

CREAM TOPPING

1 cup heavy cream, cold

½ tablespoon honey

SHORTCAKE

2½ cups all-purpose flour

¼ cup granulated sugar

2 teaspoons baking powder

1 teaspoon baking soda

½ teaspoon coarse salt

½ cup unsalted butter, cubed (1 stick), plus
    1 teaspoon to coat pan

1 cup buttermilk

The berry mixture: Wash all berries, using a colander.

Pour in vinegar and mix well. Sprinkle with sugar and salt. Combine well.

Cover and let stand for a minimum of 30 minutes. Overnight is fine.

The cream topping: Pour cream and honey into a large chilled bowl.

Whip cream and honey, using a hand mixer, stand mixer, or whisk. For better results, chill the whipping equipment.

The cream should have soft peaks.

The shortcake: Preheat the oven to 400°F.

In a large bowl, add the dry ingredients. Whisk together to combine. Add the butter and cut into the dry ingredients. Cut until the ingredients are incorporated in pea-sized lumps.

Make a well in the center of the bowl. Add ½ cup of the buttermilk to the well. Using your hands, gently incorporate the buttermilk into the biscuits. Add additional buttermilk and continue to gently mix together.

Flour your surface and add the biscuit batter. Gently knead 1 to 2 turns. Roll out to 1-inch thickness. Cut into 3-inch circles. Using 1 teaspoon butter, grease two 9-inch cake pans. Place the biscuits into the pan, touching. Bake for 15 minutes, until golden brown.

Build the dessert by cutting the shortcake horizontally. Scoop 3 tablespoons of fruit over the shortcake. Then, top with 3 tablespoons of cream. Garnish with mint, if desired.

Fruits and Nuts

Southern saying: "The fruit don't fall too far from the tree."

Dr. George Washington Carver is best known as the peanut man, botanist, and director of experiment stations at Tuskegee University in Macon County, Alabama. He wrote and distributed 44 bulletins or manuals for farmers on how to maintain crops and creatively use them in recipes. My favorite editions are *No. 12 Saving the Wild Plum Crop* and *No. 31 How to Grow the Peanut & 105 Ways of Preparing it for Human Consumption.*

Dr. Carver patented only three of his concepts and freely advised rural growers on crop rotation. In 1943, he left his life's savings (a little less than a million dollars) to further agricultural research—generous.

Dried Peaches and Cacao Nib Chocolate Bark

You can have your candy and eat it too. I found pure joy in taking a handful of coins and buying Boston Baked Beans and Butterfingers from stores operated by Tony Cook and Mrs. White. Both ran old-timey general stores located a few streets over from my childhood home. A luscious piece of chocolate with all the right notes and textures still makes me happy.

Feeds 10

19½ ounces 70% dark chocolate, chopped
1 cup dried peaches, sliced (see note)
1 teaspoon cacao nibs
½ teaspoon coarse salt

Place the dark chocolate over a double boiler with simmering water on medium-low heat. Stand close by and stir regularly. Once the chocolate looks mostly melted, remove from heat and stir a few more times.

Line a 17 × 12-inch jelly roll pan with parchment paper. Pour and spread out the chocolate. Scatter the peaches over the chocolate. Sprinkle in the cacao nibs and salt.

Refrigerate for three hours, or until set. Remove from pan and break into large pieces.

Transfer to an airtight container; the bark will keep for a few days.

Note: Using a dehydrator to dry your own fruit is an option here. Otherwise, I suggest buying dried peaches and other fruit in bulk.

Spiced Nuts

My mother always tells me "at Christmastime, we got shoeboxes of fruits, nuts, and peppermint." In fact, my holidays aren't complete without dotting a centerpiece of citrus with candy canes and fresh nuts. I can count on Aunt Jean to supply me with a heap of pecans and a piece of their childhood.

Feeds 4–6

1 cup Brazil nuts, whole (¼ pound)
1 cup pecans, halves (¼ pound)
½ tablespoon whole mustard seeds
4 tablespoons unsalted butter
¼ cup dark brown sugar, packed
½ tablespoon crushed red pepper
½ teaspoon ground cinnamon
1 teaspoon coarse salt
½ tablespoon smoked paprika

Toast Brazil nuts and pecans in a 12-inch skillet over medium-low heat. Toss nuts around for 10 minutes. Remove from flame and set aside in small mixing bowl.

Crush mustard seeds, using a mortar and pestle. Set aside.

Add butter and brown sugar to same skillet, over medium-low heat. When butter is melted, add crushed red pepper, mustard seeds, cinnamon, salt, and paprika. Stir until golden brown, about 5 minutes.

Add the entire mixing bowl of nuts to the skillet and coat well.

Transfer to mixing bowl. Let cool.

Store in airtight container; the nuts will keep for a week or so.

Pecan Pie

Trees tell stories. I think about the historic magnolia tree saved by the late Hattie Carthan in Bedford-Stuyvesant, Brooklyn. I remember the pecan trees planted by my grandfather over 50 years ago. One is still standing and is the center of a public park in my hometown. Generations continue to reap the benefits of a selfless act.

Feeds 16

1 (9-inch) Butter Pie Crust (see recipe, page 156)
6 large eggs, lightly beaten
1 cup granulated sugar
½ cup light brown sugar
1 cup dark corn syrup
2 teaspoon vanilla paste
2 tablespoons bourbon
½ teaspoon coarse salt
½ cup butter (1 stick)
3 cups coarsely chopped pecans (¾ pound)

Preheat oven to 325°F.

Roll pie dough into one 9-inch pie pan. Set aside in the fridge.

Combine eggs, sugars, and corn syrup, using a wire whisk, stand mixer, or hand mixer.

Stir in vanilla paste and bourbon. Sprinkle in salt.

Melt butter and transfer to egg and sugar mixture. Fold in pecans.

Transfer filling to pie crust.

Place in middle rack position of oven for 1 hour. Place a jelly roll pan on the lower rack to catch any spillage.

The center of pie should bounce back when done.

Transfer to wire cooling rack. Let cool completely.

Note: I always make two pies and freeze one for an impromptu dinner party.

Concord Grape Jam

Summer camp meant two things: swimming and peanut butter and jelly sandwiches made with the deep purple, sweet stuff. I had a conversation with North Carolina native and food competition queen Emily Hanhan about the first time tasting a real concord grape jam versus the grape spread of our childhood. I asked for her recipe.

Makes 2 cups

1 pound Concord grapes
½ cup red wine
1½ cups granulated sugar, plus ½ cup (optional, see note)
1 tablespoon plus 1½ teaspoons lemon juice (½ lemon)
Small pinch coarse salt

Rinse your grapes thoroughly. Remove the grapes from the stems and rinse a second time.

Separate the grape guts from the grape skins. Set up two bowls on your counter. Grab a grape from the opposite end of where it was attached to the stem. Pinch the grape, letting the green grape innards go into one bowl. Put the purple grape skins in the second bowl. Continue this until all grapes are separated.

In a heavy-bottom saucepan, add the grape skins, wine, sugar, lemon juice, and salt. Bring to a boil at medium-high heat. Once boiling, turn the heat down to medium, cooking at a steady simmer for 10–15 minutes.

While the grape skins are cooking, strain the seeds from the grape guts. A food mill is the best tool for this task, but you can also achieve this by forcing the grapes through a fine sieve.

Add the seedless grape innards to the grape skins, turn the heat to medium-high, and bring the mixture back to a boil. Once at a rolling boil, turn the heat back down to medium and cook at a slow simmer for 15 minutes.

Let the mixture cool for 3–5 minutes and then transfer to heat-proof containers. The jam will store in the refrigerator for at least 4 weeks.

Note: Sugar amount varies depending on your preferred sweetness. The lesser amount will give a more complex flavor. The higher amount will give you a sweeter flavor, closer to "childhood grape jelly."

Plum Cake

This simple cake is my "I'm trying to impress people" dessert. After the death of my father, I developed a relationship with my paternal aunts and half-siblings. I invited the Dillard/Shorter family down from Philadelphia, and my tiny apartment became an all-day brunch spot. The two plum cakes were a hit. Use a heavy stock paper to cut out cursive wording, or use cut pieces of paper to do a gorgeous design. Lay these patterns on the cake and dust on the powdered sugar. Then carefully remove the paper patterns. Not that creative? Just dust powdered sugar on top of cake with a duster.

Feeds 8

6 medium plums (around 1 pound)

2 cups all-purpose flour, plus 1 teaspoon to coat pan

1 teaspoon baking powder

¼ teaspoon ground cinnamon

⅓ teaspoon baking soda

½ cup unsalted butter (1 stick), plus 1 tablespoon to coat pan

½ cup granulated sugar

2 large eggs

½ cup buttermilk

1 teaspoon vanilla paste

½ cup powdered sugar (optional)

Preheat oven to 350°F.

Rinse and remove any dirt from plums. Cut in half and pit. Set aside.

Combine flour, baking powder, cinnamon, and baking soda in a large bowl. Whisk well and set aside.

Cream butter and sugar, using paddle attachment of stand mixer or a hand mixer. Add eggs, buttermilk, and vanilla paste. Gradually incorporate the flour mixture on low speed. Combine but don't overbeat.

Butter and flour a 9-inch springform pan. Pour batter into pan.

Strategically place plums (skin side buried) in batter.

Place cake in middle rack position of oven. Bake for 45 minutes.

Transfer to wire cooling rack. Let cool completely.

Apple Crisp

I've always enjoyed roaming outdoors and picking fruit. My childhood neighborhood was full of crab apple trees, but all the kids were warned to eat only one because having more would make you deathly sick. Truth is, crab apples are fine to eat when ripe. My favorite varieties for baking that are special to New York State are Cortland, Empire, and McIntosh.

Feeds 6–8

4 cups apples (about 2 pounds)
3 tablespoons lemon juice (1 lemon)
¼ teaspoon cardamom
¼ teaspoon ground ginger
¼ teaspoon nutmeg
¼ teaspoon cinnamon
½ teaspoon coarse salt
¼ teaspoon vanilla paste
5 dashes Angostura bitters (optional)
½ cup granulated sugar
½ cup dark brown sugar
1½ cups all-purpose flour
½ cup benne flour
¾ cup unsalted butter (1½ sticks)

Preheat oven to 400°F.

Peel and core apples. If you have access to wild crab apples, combine two cups with a pound of popular apples and sprinkle with two teaspoons of sugar. Cut in rough half-moon shapes. Squeeze the lemon juice over cut pieces. Place in a large bowl.

Sprinkle cardamom, ginger, nutmeg, cinnamon, and salt over apples. Stir well. Pour in vanilla paste. Transfer to 7 × 11-inch pan. Sprinkle with bitters and set aside.

Combine granulated sugar, brown sugar, and flours. Mix very well. Set aside.

Melt butter over low heat, using a saucier. Transfer melted butter to sugar and flour mixture. Combine well; the color will be a lush dark brown. Cover and place in the fridge for a minimum of 20 minutes.

Remove sugar and flour mixture from fridge. Fluff with fork and evenly sprinkle over apples.

Bake for 40 minutes.

Pecan-Buckwheat Shortbread

The word buckwheat takes me back to *The Little Rascals* character Billie "Buckwheat" Thomas. The TV series never mentioned the ancient pseudo-grain pancakes or Japanese soba noodles that are made with buckwheat. I always buy a small quantity of buckwheat and mix it into my favorite desserts. It provides a deep, earthy flavor.

Feeds 12

½ cup coarsely chopped pecans
¼ cup brown sugar, packed
¼ cup granulated sugar
1½ cups unsalted butter (3 sticks)
1 teaspoon vanilla paste
1½ cups buckwheat flour
1½ cups all-purpose flour, plus 1 teaspoon to roll out dough
½ teaspoon coarse salt

Preheat your oven to 325°F.

Toss pecans in a 12-inch skillet, over medium heat. Shake skillet a bit to move nuts around. Toast for about 10 minutes. Set aside.

Cream together brown sugar, granulated sugar, and butter, using the paddle on a stand mixer or a hand mixer. Pour and stir in the vanilla paste.

Mix together both flours and add salt. Slowly incorporate flour mixture into creamed butter. Don't overmix, just combine.

Pour in pecans.

Sprinkle surface with 1 teaspoon of flour.

Transfer shortbread to surface, using a pastry scraper. A tip here is to place pastry scraper and rolling pin in the freezer before using.

Gently knead 1 to 2 turns with your rolling pin. Roll out to ½ inch thickness.

continued

Dip shortbread cutter into your container of all-purpose flour; this helps with a flawless cut. Press cutter in dough.

Place the cut shortbread onto a Silpat (a nonstick baking mat) or parchment-lined jelly roll pan. The shortbread should be a minimum of 2 inches apart.

Gently place 3 holes in the shortbread pieces, using a skewer.

Place in middle rack position of oven. Bake for 45 minutes.

Transfer to cooling rack.

Note: Purchase only small quantities of buckwheat because the shelf life is short.

Blackberry Cobbler

My goal here was to re-create the blackberry cobbler at Busy Bee Cafe in Atlanta. The restaurant has been around since 1947 and was a skip, hop, and a jump from my dorm during my freshman and sophomore years in college. Nothing compares to the dessert from my all-time favorite soul food restaurant, but this recipe is damn good and almost better than the cobbler at "the Bee."

Feeds 6–8

PASTRY TOPPING

¾ cup unsalted butter (1½ sticks)

2 cups all-purpose flour, plus 1 teaspoon
    for rolling dough

½ teaspoon coarse salt

¼ cup cold water

¼ cup buttermilk

BLACKBERRY COBBLER

4 cups fresh or frozen blackberries (1¼
    pounds)

2 teaspoons lemon juice (about ½ lemon)

1½ teaspoons cornstarch

½ cup granulated sugar, plus 3 tablespoons
    to sprinkle on top

¼ teaspoon coarse salt

4 dashes Angostura bitters

1 egg

The topping: For the best topping, I place the butter and pastry blender in the freezer while mixing the flour and salt. Cold ingredients and utensils help achieve a flaky pastry.

In a large mixing bowl, combine flour and salt. Using the pastry blender, cut the butter into the flour.

When the mixture resembles sand with lumps, sprinkle in water and buttermilk. Bring the mass of dough together. Lightly flour a surface.

Transfer dough to surface, using a pastry scraper.

Flour a large flat surface. Using a rolling pin, roll out dough into a 10-inch circle. The dough will be a bit sticky. Gently knead 1 to 2 turns with your pin.

Scoop dough onto parchment paper and press into a flat round. Wrap tightly and place in the fridge for about an hour.

continued

The blackberry cobbler: Preheat oven to 325°F.

Combine fruit, lemon juice, cornstarch, ½ cup sugar, salt, and bitters in a large mixing bowl. Stir well.

Transfer berry mixture to 11 × 7-inch baking dish.

Roll the pastry topping out into a square shape (¼ inch thick). The pastry will be slightly sticky.

Cut pastry into strips and place over the berries. The pastry should have a rustic appearance.

Crack and beat an egg. Whisk in ½ tablespoon of water. Paint egg wash over the crust with a pastry brush. This will help achieve a golden crust.

Place on the middle rack in the oven and bake for 40 minutes.

Sprinkle remaining sugar on top of cobbler.

Let cool a bit before serving.

Nectarine and Blueberry Compote and Plain Ice Cream

I've learned so much about the way my family lived on the land. My late grandfather Boley had the biggest garden in the neighborhood and was unselfish with his entire harvest. I'll be honest, fruit prices are rising and fruit is the one thing I'm likely not to share.

Makes 4 cups

ICE CREAM
5 large egg yolks
6 tablespoons whole milk
1¾ cups heavy cream
6 tablespoons buttermilk
½ cup granulated sugar
¼ teaspoon coarse salt
2 teaspoons vanilla paste

COMPOTE
2 cups diced nectarines (1 pound)
1 cup fresh blueberries (⅓ pound)
¼ cup dark rum
¼ cup water
3 tablespoons granulated sugar
Small pinch coarse salt

The ice cream: Crack and separate yolk and whites from eggs; use two large bowls. Refrigerate whites.

Whisk yolks well.

Combine milk, cream, buttermilk, sugar, and salt in heavy medium saucepan over medium-high heat.

Watch and whisk cream mixture. Don't let the cream mixture boil. If you notice rapid bubbles, reduce the heat.

Next, temper the egg yolks by spooning about a cup of cream mixture into bowl of yolks. Reduce flame to medium-low heat.

Whisk egg and warm cream base mixture well.

Slowly pour egg-yolk mixture back into cream base saucepan, over medium-low heat.

Add vanilla paste. Gingerly stir with spoon. Watch and stir.

The cream base is ready when it coats the spoon but doesn't stick. The base should not be like broth or yogurt. The appearance should be something in the middle.

Strain the ice cream into a chilled bowl or container. The base needs to cool down completely before transferring. Once at room temperature, cover and transfer to freezer for a minimum of 2 hours.

Complete the ice-cream-making process by following the directions of your ice cream maker.

When ready, the ice cream will be soft. You can serve immediately or transfer to a loaf pan and store in freezer.

Scoop out and enjoy with compote.

The compote: Combine nectarines, blueberries, rum, water, sugar, and salt in medium saucepan over medium-high heat. Mix well.

Stir a few times while mixture thickens. Cook for about 20 minutes, until compote comes together. The compote should fall off the spoon with a slight shake.

Let cool a little and serve warm over ice cream.

Note: This compote is also a perfect topping for the Lemon Pound Cake (see page 139).

Watermelon and Lime Salt

In the rural South, saving newspapers wasn't a mandate from a city's recycling program. Newspapers got saved because they were essential to serving food. Children could never eat watermelon inside. Instead, we were summoned to the back porch with a giant chunk of watermelon on a fold of newspaper.

Makes ½ cup

½ cup coarse salt
1½ teaspoons lime zest (about 1 lime)
Watermelon

Combine salt and lime zest for a minimum of 24 hours. Transfer to airtight container.

Cut watermelon into slices with rind attached.

Sprinkle desired amount of lime salt.

Benne and Banana Sandwich Cookies

Benne is the colonial-period version of sesame. You probably will be unable to find benne in your local supermarket, but if you have a garden, you can try planting it. Many catalogs that carry heirloom varieties have the seeds.

The key to this filling is to use excellent butter. If your banana isn't ripe, place it in a low-heat oven (around 200°F) for a minimum of 30 minutes. The fruit will need to cool before making the buttercream.

Feeds 12

COOKIES

¾ cup sesame seeds, toasted
1 cup plus 2 tablespoons unsalted butter
   (2¼ sticks)
½ cup light brown sugar, packed
½ cup granulated sugar
½ teaspoon vanilla paste
1 large egg
1 cup all-purpose flour
⅓ cup benne flour
¼ teaspoon baking soda
¼ teaspoon coarse salt

BANANA BUTTERCREAM FILLING

½ ripe banana, sliced
½ cup unsalted butter, softened (1 stick)
¼ teaspoon vanilla paste
Small pinch or 1 teaspoon coarse salt
1½ cups powdered sugar

The cookies: Preheat oven to 350°F. Toast the sesame seeds on medium-low for 6 minutes, until golden brown.

Cream the butter and sugars together on medium heat for about 3 minutes, or until light and fluffy. Add the vanilla paste and egg and beat for another minute.

With the mixer on low speed, add the all-purpose and benne flours, baking soda, salt, and sesame seeds. Stir until just combined.

Line 2 baking sheets with parchment or Silpat (nonstick baking mat). Using a medium ice cream scoop or a tablespoon, dollop the batter onto the sheets, 12 cookies per pan. Using damp hands, press the cookies down until they are about 1½ inches in diameter.

Bake on top rack of oven for 6 minutes, until golden brown.

Let the cookies sit on a rack until completely cool.

The banana buttercream filling: Place the banana, butter, vanilla paste, and salt into a stand mixer bowl. Beat on medium speed for 3–4 minutes, until light and fluffy. Slowly add the powdered sugar to the mixture as the machine is still running. Once the sugar is fully incorporated, turn the mixer off and scrape the sides of the bowl.

Turn the mixer back on medium speed and beat for a few more minutes.

Spread 2 tablespoons of banana buttercream on one side of half the cookies. Place the bottom sides of the other half of the cookies on top of the buttercream sides.

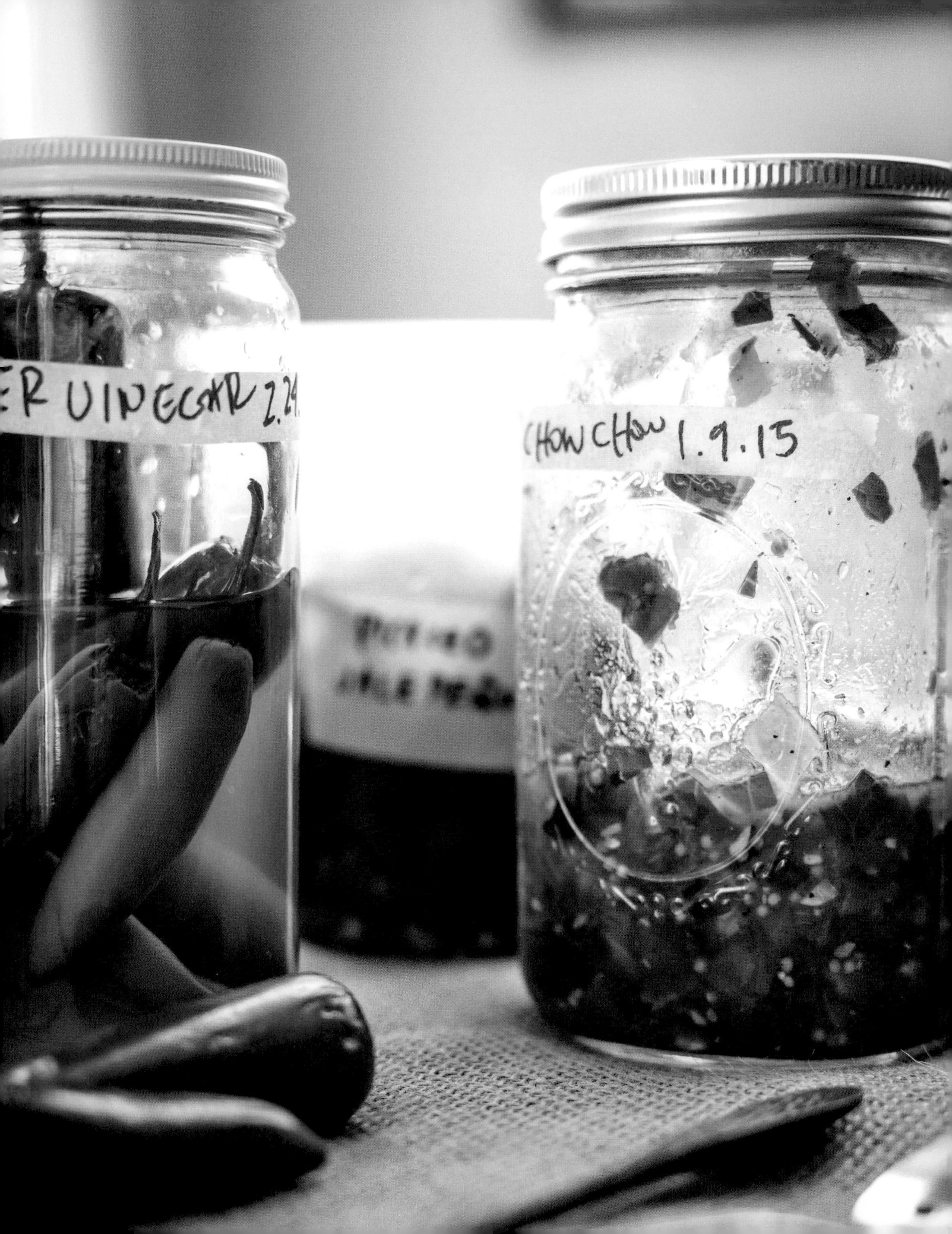
ER VINEGAR 2.24.
CHOW CHOW 1.9.15

Chow Chow and Garnishes

Southern saying: "Feed 'em with a long-handled spoon."

I asked my friend and culinary historian Michael Twitty to give me a lesson on the silent stars of the Southern plate. This is what he had to say:

In the South, the inevitable constraints of seasonality and monotony were broken by the custom of enjoying food with a relish. Originally "relish," from the Middle English via French for "remains," as used in the South, didn't just refer to tasty condiments enjoyed with food. A salt herring might be a relish for an ashcake or a bit of wild salad or greens for rice or cornbread. As West and Central African, British, French, and German cultures blended in the South, the repertoire of condiments grew. The African preference for hot and peppery condiments not only spurred a love of hot sauce, but it inspired extra zing in chow chows. The lack of vegetables in the winter was broken by gourds, crocks, and jars bearing treats from past harvests.

Chow Chow

What's chow chow? A mix of finely chopped pickled vegetables that are parked in the door of the fridge. The main ingredient is cabbage, and most everything else is free-style. It took me years, and coming up with my own recipe, to appreciate this condiment. I like a chunky chow chow, but feel free to use a food processor for a smoother texture. Add a spoonful to a serving of greens or bread.

Makes 3 cups

1½ cups cabbage, chopped (about ⅓ head of cabbage)

1½ cups chopped green pepper (about 1½ large peppers)

1½ cups chopped green tomato (about 2 medium green tomatoes)

1 cup white vinegar

½ cup granulated sugar

⅓ cup chopped onions (about ½ small onion)

⅓ cup finely chopped celery (about 2 ribs)

⅓ cup chopped cucumber (about ½ medium cucumber)

3 garlic cloves, minced (about 1½ teaspoons)

1 small chopped hot pepper, deseeded

1 tablespoon coarse salt

1½ teaspoons yellow mustard seeds

½ teaspoon mustard powder

½ teaspoon ground black pepper

Combine all ingredients in a large bowl. Set aside in the fridge for 2 hours minimum or overnight.

Remove from fridge. Drain the mixture, separating vegetables from the liquid. Reserve liquid.

In a medium saucepan on medium heat, bring the vegetables to a simmer. Reduce heat to low, and cover the pot for 45 minutes. There should be very little liquid in the pot and the mixture should be soft but not mushy.

Add about half the reserved liquid to the pot. The chow chow shouldn't be swimming in liquid.

Mix well. Turn flame off, cover, and let cool.

Transfer to airtight container and place in fridge.

Pickled Onions

In my neck of the woods, many things are topped with pickled onions. Grits and sandwiches get a dose. Keep a full container on hand to liven up the simplest of meals.

Makes 2 cups

1 cup water

1 cup white vinegar

2 teaspoons coarse salt

¼ cup granulated sugar

2 cups thinly sliced onions (about 2 medium onions)

Combine the water, vinegar, salt, and sugar in a large wide-mouth mason jar. Combine well.

Place onions inside.

Seal jar and refrigerate. Their shelf life is around 2 weeks.

Pickled Hot Peppers

BK Swappers is both a larder swap and a social gathering. Gangs of folks (mostly Brooklyn food fanatics) bring delights in mason jars and goodies wrapped in linen to exchange. In 2010, I attended the first one and exchanged biscuits for pickled hot peppers.

Makes 2 cups

2 cups sliced jalapeños (about ½ pound)

1 cup water

1 cup white vinegar

1 teaspoon whole black peppercorns

2 teaspoons coarse salt

3 garlic cloves

¼ cup granulated sugar

1 dried bay leaf

Rinse and remove any dirt from peppers. Slice to desired thickness (I prefer ⅛-inch size). Another option is to cut the peppers vertically. Set aside.

Combine the water and vinegar in a large wide-mouth mason jar. Add peppercorns, salt, garlic cloves, sugar, and bay leaf. Combine well. Place peppers inside.

Seal jar and refrigerate. Their shelf life is about 2 weeks.

Pickled Ramps

Ramps have a very short season, so putting them up makes sense. These wild onions scream for a place on a Southern cheese plate.

Makes 1 pint

2 bunches ramps, white bottoms only
 (about 1 pound)
¾ cup water
6 tablespoons apple cider vinegar
6 tablespoons rice vinegar
1 teaspoon coarse salt
½ teaspoon whole black peppercorns
¼ teaspoon red pepper flakes
2 whole allspice berries

Rinse and remove any dirt from ramps. Cut away green tops and set aside. Place ramp whites in large wide-mouth mason jar.

Combine the water and vinegars in a medium heavy saucepan on high heat. Add salt, peppercorns, red pepper flakes, and allspice berries. Cover the saucepan and bring to a boil. Remove from flame and let cool for 30 minutes. (Cooling the liquid first prevents the ramps from cooking or softening.)

Pour the liquid over the ramps and seal jar. Store in fridge. Their shelf life is about 2 weeks.

Note: The reserved green ramp tops can be used in dishes to replace garlic or onions.

Hot Pepper Vinegar

My appreciation for garnishes developed late in life. This was my gateway condiment.

Makes 1 cup

6 hot peppers
½ cup white vinegar
½ cup apple cider vinegar
1 teaspoon coarse salt

Place peppers in a large wide-mouth mason jar. Set aside.

Combine the vinegars and salt in a medium heavy saucepan on high heat. Cover the saucepan and bring to a boil.

Remove from flame and let cool for 30 minutes. Pour mixture over peppers.

Seal jar and let sit a few days. At this time you can transfer the vinegar to a jar; this will allow easy dashes on food. The whole peppers can be transferred to another container and used as a garnish.

Cucumber and Onion Salad

It's a pleasure to meet folks with the same quirks. Longtime Bedford-Stuyvesant neighborhood resident and pioneering salon owner Anu Prestonia requested a separate plate for her veggies and protein. Like me, she prefers her food not to touch or run together immediately.

Feeds 4–6

½ cup sliced onion (about ½ medium onion)

2 cups sliced cucumbers (about 1 large cucumber)

½ cup white vinegar

1 teaspoon granulated sugar

½ teaspoon coarse salt

¼ teaspoon ground white pepper

Peel the half onion. Slice cucumber and onion, using a mandoline or slicer to ¼-inch size.

Pour the vinegar on the vegetables. Then, sprinkle the sugar, salt, and pepper. Combine well.

Cover and set aside for 1 hour.

Fried Green Tomatoes

On June 19, 1865, two years after President Lincoln's Emancipation Proclamation became official, enslaved people in Galveston, Texas were told they were free. Since the mid-nineteenth century, black communities across the nation have celebrated their culture, freedom, and accomplishments with a festive fete—Juneteenth. To keep the tradition, I host an annual feast with green tomatoes making the menu.

Feeds 2–4

- 2 large green tomatoes (1 pound), cleaned and sliced into ½-inch slices
- 1 teaspoon plus ¼ teaspoon coarse salt, divided
- 1 teaspoon plus ¼ teaspoon ground black pepper, divided
- ¾ cup buttermilk
- ½ cup fine cornmeal
- ½ cup all-purpose flour
- ¼ teaspoon onion powder
- ¼ teaspoon smoked paprika
- ¼ teaspoon red pepper flakes
- 1½ cups sunflower oil

Sprinkle tomato slices with 1 teaspoon salt and 1 teaspoon pepper, pour buttermilk into a shallow bowl. Place the tomatoes in and soak for 15 minutes.

Combine ¼ teaspoon salt, ¼ teaspoon pepper, cornmeal, flour, onion powder, smoked paprika, and red pepper flakes in a large bowl. Whisk well. Dredge both sides of the tomatoes in the mixture.

Place oil in a large skillet over high heat. Heat until an instant-read thermometer reads 350°F.

Carefully drop tomatoes in the oil (work in batches). Cook about a minute on each side or until golden brown. Remember to let the oil reach the 350°F mark before dropping more fritters, and don't crowd the pan.

Transfer to jelly roll sheet with cooling rack on top.

Note: Boost the flavor with a dollop of basil goat cheese. Mix together 4 ounces goat cheese or chevre and 3 shredded fresh basil leaves. Finish with a small pinch of black pepper. Top a few tomatoes with the mixture.

Whitelikker and Sweet Tea

Southern saying: "The likker is talkin'."

Honestly, the bearded hipsters and reality TV bootlegger stars are 180 degrees different from the booze pushers I remember in Athens, Georgia. They were all ladies. One sang in the church choir, another lived in a brick house with a long driveway, and another was a neighbor on the next street. It seemed normal to me that the people who sold whitelikker were respected and even had day jobs.

Whitelikker was made in the country. It was the large clear jug that fascinated me. The special potion hidden at the bottom of kitchen cabinets and only brought out for esteemed guests. It was like the good china.

Up until recently, Athens was a dry-on-Sunday town, meaning restaurants or bars did not sell alcohol on Sundays. By the 1980s, the bootleggers I saw in Athens were buying it wholesale from smaller surrounding counties and selling it to the old-school folks. Having a stash of what some would call moonshine was as normal as keeping a pitcher of sweet tea in the fridge.

I think of these women, renegade entrepreneurs, when I visit NYC liquor stores and browse the rows of small-batch spirits that started off in studio apartments and are now being distributed all over the United States, often accompanied with a flashy beverage book. These women were the first distributors to me—part of an elite group that everyone wanted to know because of their goods—whitelikker.

Thyme Simple Syrup

Your thyme should be a bright color and fragrant before you make this syrup.

Makes 3 cups

2 cups granulated sugar

4 cups water

1 bunch fresh thyme (around 8 sprigs)

2 teaspoon lime zest (about 1 lime)

Place sugar and water in a medium saucepan, over medium-high heat. The sugar will dissolve in about 5 minutes.

Place fresh thyme and lime zest in sugar mixture.

Turn flame off, cover, and let cool. Discard thyme.

Transfer to airtight container and place in fridge.

Thyme Limeade

All I can manage in our fourth-floor walk-up apartment are windowsill herbs. I started the project after being gifted leftover plants from my first New York friend, Adriana Velez. I've started and stopped this project so many times because every time I go out of town, I forget to recruit a "plant sitter." Last year, I embarked on the project again and was successful with thyme.

Pours 8

¾ cup lemon juice (from about 4 lemons)

1½ cups lime juice (from about 8 limes)

4 cups water

1½ cups Thyme Simple Syrup
   (see page 203)

Ice

Thyme sprig (optional)

Cut lemons and limes in half. Using a citrus extractor or hands, squeeze the citrus and set aside.

Add juice, water, and simple syrup to standard-sized pitcher (64 ounces). Stir well. Refrigerate.

Pour over desired amount of ice, using your favorite glass or mason jar. Garnish with thyme sprig.

Note: Store the squeezed lemon and lime leftovers in the freezer and add to roast chicken (see Whole Roasted Bird, page 92) or roasted duck (see Whole Roasted Duck and Cherries, page 100).

Honeysuckle Sparkler

Fondly, I remember honeysuckles in my backyard when I was growing up. Having fun meant picking the gentle bud and tasting the inside stem. Honeysuckles grow on a climbing shrub and the sweet smell lingers. If you don't have a bush, purchase the dried version online or in specialty stores.

Pours 2

3 ounces Honeysuckle Simple Syrup (see page 207)
8 ounces sparkling water
Ice (optional)

To make the sparkler, place 1½ ounces of syrup into two collins or highball glasses. Top both with sparkling water. Stir well with a bar spoon.

Place a few cubes of ice in glass, if you wish.

Honeysuckle Simple Syrup

There are plenty of simple syrups on the market, but I've never seen honeysuckle in the mix. This is something special.

Makes 2 cups

3 cups fresh honeysuckles or 2 cups dried

1½ cups lukewarm water

½ cup Turbinado Simple Syrup (see recipe, page 210)

Place the honeysuckles in cheesecloth and tie with kitchen twine.

Pour water and honeysuckle bunch in a large bowl. Cover with kitchen towel. Let steep for a minimum of 1 hour. For best results, steep overnight.

Remove bunch from water. Strain to remove any pieces of the honeysuckles.

Add turbinado simple syrup.

Transfer to airtight container and place in fridge.

Sweet Tea

The key to excellent sweet tea is good ol' water and quality loose-leaf black tea. I'm fond of Gullah Girl Tea's Full Moon at the Sands blend. The owner of Gullah Girl Tea, Charmaine Bee, is from Beaufort, South Carolina and now lives a block away from me. My mama reminded me that Southerners add a pinch of baking soda to make the perfect pitcher.

Pours 8

7 cups boiling water
½ cup loose black tea
¼ teaspoon baking soda
1 cup Turbinado Simple Syrup
    (see recipe, page 210)
Ice
Lemon wedges (optional)

Place water in a medium saucepan, over medium-high heat. After coming to a boiling, drop in cheesecloth (tied with kitchen twine) or infuser filled with loose tea.

Turn off heat. Cover and let brew for 10 minutes.

Add baking soda and syrup. Stir well. Transfer to standard-sized pitcher (64 ounces). Refrigerate.

Pour over desired amount of ice. Garnish with lemon wedge.

Store in fridge.

Q&A WITH GULLAH GIRL TEA

Charmaine Bee is keeping her corner of the American South alive through her company, Gullah Girl Tea, and her original blends and tinctures.

Give me the 411 on your connection to "down south."

I was born in New York and raised in Beaufort. Beaufort is situated on the coast of South Carolina (45 minutes from Savannah, Georgia and a little over an hour away from Charleston). That's where my mother, grandmother, and grandmother's father were born.

How did your childhood backyard and local farmers influence Gullah Girl Tea?

In terms of farmers, I guess I remember the relationship that they had with my grandmother and other family members, and how local access was. Sometimes there would be folks selling collard greens, watermelon, or okra out of the back of their trucks on the side of the road. Or my grandmother knew just the spot to go get these items, and they all knew her and there was this organic and rich relationship of staying connected through this exchange of food grown not too far from where she lived. She also passed this on to my mother and her siblings.

My grandmother gave birth to all of her children in the house and the placentas were buried on the land. She would go near the area, pull horehound, and make herbal infusions for healing.

So, how does this all influence Gullah Girl Tea?

Well, the stories, the connectedness that happens over a cup of tea, a lot of that I draw from home. I'd love for Gullah Girl to encourage folks to sit down and remember their stories and create new ones.

Turbinado Simple Syrup

All simple syrups will last several weeks in the fridge. You can use granulated sugar in place of regular (turbinado) sugar for all the drink recipes in this book.

Feel free to substitute agave syrup where you see granulated or turbinado sugar. If you use agave, you'll need to half the amount. Agave is a real sugar made from a spiky plant that's mostly found in Mexico.

Makes 2½ cups

1 cup turbinado sugar
2 cups water

Place sugar and water in a medium saucepan, over medium-high heat. The sugar will dissolve in about 5 minutes.

Turn flame off, cover, and let cool.

Transfer to airtight container and place in fridge.

Eggnog

Today, the University of Georgia Creamery exists as a dining hall for college students. But in the 1980s it was the place to purchase ice cream, punch, and other premium dairy, made on the premises. I thought that was the be-all and end-all of eggnog, until I made my own. Buying the best ingredients will keep your holiday guests asking for more.

Pours 7

4 large eggs, separated
⅓ cup granulated sugar
3 cups half-and-half
1½ cups heavy cream
1 teaspoon vanilla paste
2 teaspoons ground nutmeg
¼ teaspoon coarse salt
White rum (optional)

Crack and separate eggs, yolks from whites. Place in two separate large bowls. Refrigerate whites.

Whisk together yolks and sugar, the color will be golden. Add half-and-half and cream. Whisk well. Pour in vanilla paste, nutmeg, salt, and rum, if using.

Remove chilled egg whites from fridge. Using a hand whisk or stand mixer (whisk attachment), mix whites until soft peaks form. The whites will look bendable.

Fold in whites with cream mixture. Transfer to a container. Refrigerate for 2 hours minimum or overnight.

New Age Church Punch

Punch bowls remind me of happy times. The gorgeous etched vessels are a symbol of celebration. They have a grown-up and mature feel, and reveal that one understands life and the art of entertaining. When I feel like having "church" or gathering friends, I pull out the bowl. My first bowl was a Bodum College Bowl Set. Famed food writer and historian Jessica B. Harris gifted me her mother's mid-century centerpiece—I cherish it.

Pours 16

2 cups roasted pineapple juice (from about one 2-pound whole pineapple)

¼ teaspoon coarse salt

½ teaspoon ground ginger

1 teaspoon brown sugar

8 cups boiling water

2 cups hibiscus leaves

1¾ cups granulated sugar

1 cup fresh lime juice (about 3 limes)

1½ cups white rum (optional)

4½ cups ginger beer, or 36 ounces

3 scoops lime sorbet (optional)

Preheat oven to 400°F.

Cut the top and bottom of pineapple. Next, sit the fruit upright and cut down the sides. Flip the pineapple on its side cut in half.

Cut into ½-inch round slices. Sprinkle pineapple slices with salt, ginger, and brown sugar. Place slices on parchment paper or Silpat (nonstick baking mat) on baking sheet or jelly roll pan. Roast for 25 minutes.

Transfer pineapple slices to Vitamix or food processor, pulse until liquid is loose and foamy. The fragrance will be bright. Set aside.

Place water in a large stockpot, over medium-high heat. After coming to a boiling, drop in hibiscus leaves. Cover and let brew for 10 minutes.

Stir in sugar and turn off heat. Let completely cool.

Add lime juice, pineapple, rum, and ginger beer. Stir well. Transfer to punch bowl.

Place scoops of lime sorbet in punch bowl, if desired. The mixture will slightly foam. The sorbet will make the punch a tad sweeter.

Stone Fruit White Sangria

Warm weather is perfect for making memories, watching sunsets, and devouring juicy peaches. By late summer, I buy copious amounts of bruised fruit and take to infusing booze, because it's the easiest way to give fruit a new life and create layered flavors in a jar. I once played bartender for a Red Hook, Brooklyn rooftop fete. My objectives were to make the transport seamless and to offer sangria among the other libations. Chilled wine was already waiting at the party, and upon arrival I simply added it to my other ingredients. No ice is needed for this beverage.

Pours 6

3 small plums (⅓ pound)

10 medium peaches (2½ pounds)

¼ cup pomegranate molasses

4 basil leaves

½ whole vanilla bean

1 bottle dry sparkling wine (3 cups)

Cut and pit plums. Peel, pit, and dice peaches. Using a Vitamix or food processor, purée 1½ cups of the peaches. Set aside.

Combine pomegranate molasses, peach purée, peaches, plums, and basil leaves in a large wide-mouth mason jar.

Cut, split, and scrape half the vanilla bean pod in the jar.

If transporting or gifting, place the lid on stone fruit base and add chilled wine and basil later.

Otherwise, transfer the fruit base to a pitcher, add ice-cold wine. Mix well.

Peanut-Infused Bourbon

This small-batch infusion is an easy way to dip your toe into the fancy cocktail movement.

Makes 1 cup

1 cup unsalted peanuts
1 cup dark American whiskey

Combine peanuts and bourbon in a clean jar.

Infuse for a minimum of one week. Strain peanuts from whiskey, using cheesecloth. This will remove most of the fat from the whiskey.

Set aside peanuts for snacking.

Peanut-Apple Toddy

My husband's midnight snack is an apple with peanut butter. This drink is a riff on that treat. I recommend white oak barrel—aged corn liquor, also known as bourbon, for this recipe. A tried-and-true Southerner keeps a standard bottle of bourbon around, but hides away the good stuff for VIP houseguests.

Pours 4

6 ounces Peanut Infused Bourbon (see page 215)

3 ounces lemon juice (about 2 lemons)

2 ounces real maple syrup

4 cubes ice

4 ounces hard apple cider

Measure bourbon, using a jigger, and pour into a Boston shaker mixing glass.

Add lemon juice, syrup, and a few cubes of ice.

Place shaker tin over glass. It should be a snug fit. Shake well.

Using a bar strainer, transfer to rocks-style glasses.

Top with cider.

Note: You'll need to drink any remaining cider immediately; it goes flat.

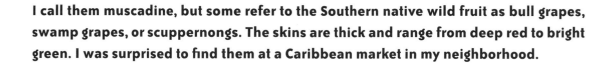

Muscadine Whitelikker Cocktail

I call them muscadine, but some refer to the Southern native wild fruit as bull grapes, swamp grapes, or scuppernongs. The skins are thick and range from deep red to bright green. I was surprised to find them at a Caribbean market in my neighborhood.

Pours 2

4 ounces white whiskey

3 ounces lemon juice (2 lemons)

3 ounces Muscadine Simple Syrup (see recipe, page 219)

Ice

2 whole muscadines, deseeded (optional)

Measure whiskey, using a jigger, and pour in a Boston shaker mixing glass.

Add lemon juice, syrup, and a few cubes of ice.

Place shaker tin over glass. It should be a snug fit. Shake well.

Using a bar strainer, transfer to coupe-style glasses.

Top each glass with a fresh muscadine.

Muscadine Simple Syrup

Make this syrup right after you buy muscadines from the farmers' market. You'll be happy to have put up muscadines after their growing season.

Makes 4 cups

2 cups muscadine grapes (about 1 pound)

1 cup granulated sugar

1 teaspoon ground cardamom

2 cups water

Place muscadines, sugar, cardamom, and water in a medium saucepan, over medium-high heat. Mix well.

The grapes will begin to burst open in about 5 minutes. To aid the process, press down on mixture (use a potato masher). Turn flame off, cover, and let completely cool.

Strain grape mixture from liquid. Transfer liquid to airtight container and place in fridge.

Muscadine Shrub

Essentially, this is a simple syrup with vinegar. This complex sweetener is great in cocktails or alone.

2 cups muscadine grapes (about 1 pound)

1 cup granulated sugar

1 teaspoon ground cardamom

2 cups water

1 cup white vinegar

Place the muscadines, sugar, cardamom, water, and vinegar in a medium saucepan, over medium-high heat. Mix well.

The grapes will begin to burst open in about 5 minutes. To aid the process, press down on mixture (use a potato masher). Turn flame off, cover, and let completely cool.

Strain grape mixture from liquid. Transfer liquid to airtight container and place in fridge.

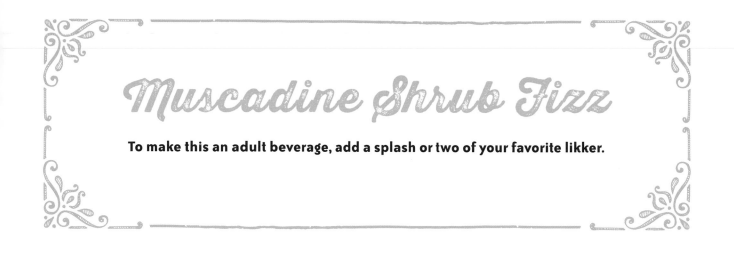

Muscadine Shrub Fizz

To make this an adult beverage, add a splash or two of your favorite likker.

Pours 2

3 ounces Muscadine Shrub (see recipe, page 220)

8 ounces seltzer

Ice (optional)

2 ounces light spirits (optional)

To make the fizz, place 1½ ounces in two collins or highball glasses. Top both with 4 ounces seltzer. Stir well with a bar spoon.

Place a few cubes of ice and spirits in glass, if you wish.

Up South Resources

I love a good treasure hunt. I'll trek all over New York City and browse the Internet to the wee hours searching for ingredients. My only requirements are speaking with a real live person and supporting businesses that believe in the power of the local economy. Once I find the perfect spot for purchases, I remain loyal.

A Cook's Companion
197 Atlantic Avenue
Brooklyn, NY 11201
718-852-6901
www.acookscompanion.com
Kitchen supplies

Anson Mills
1922 C Gervais Street
Columbia, SC 29201
803-467-4122
www.ansonmills.com
Rice, grits, Sea Island red peas,
benne, and benne flour

Astor Wines
99 Lafayette Street
New York, NY 10003
212-674-7500
www.astorwines.com
Whiskey, rum, and hard cider

Bacchanal Pepper Sauce
www.bacchanalsauce.com

Brooklyn Rescue Mission Inc.
255 Bainbridge Street
Brooklyn, NY 11233
718-363-3085
www.brooklynrescuemission.org
Farmers' markets

Brooklyn Victory Garden
920 Fulton Street
Brooklyn, NY 11238
718-398-9100
www.brooklynvictorygarden.com
Artisanal food items

Cee Bee's Citrus
16907 Boy Scout Road
Odessa, FL 33556
1-866-248-7870
www.ceebeescitrus.com

Court Street Grocers
485 Court Street
Brooklyn, NY 11231
718-722-7229
courtstreetgrocers.com
Cheerwine and Geechee Boy
Mill products

Fresh Frozen Foods
1-800-277-9851
www.freshfrozenfoods.com
Southern peas and beans

Georgia Olive Farms
P.O. Box 245
Lakeland, GA 31635
229-482-3505
www.georgiaolivefarms.com
Olive oil

The Greene Grape
767 Fulton Street
Brooklyn, NY 11217
718-233-2700
www.greenegrape.com
Sustainable meat, seafood, and
artisanal food items

Grow NYC
51 Chambers Street, Room 228
New York, NY 10007
212-788-7900
www.grownyc.org
Farmers' markets

Gullah Girl Tea
www.gullahgirltea.com
Loose-leaf tea

Heritage Foods USA
718-389-0985
www.heritagefoodsusa.com
Ducks, heritage turkeys, grass-fed
beef, and Berkshire pork

Hudson Valley Seed Library
484 Mettacahonts Road
Accord, NY 12404
845-204-8769
www.seedlibrary.org

The J. M. Clayton Company
www.jmclayton.com
Soft-shell crabs

Kalustyans's
123 Lexington Avenue
New York, NY 10016
212-685-3451
www.kalustyans.com
Kecap manis

King Arthur Flour
135 US Route 5 South
Norwich, VT 05055
1-800-827-6836
www.kingarthurflour.com

La Tourangelle
125 University Avenue
Berkeley, CA 94710
1-866-NUT-OILS
www.latourangelle.com
Sun Coco oil, sunflower oil,
coconut oil

Mills Farm's Red Mule Grits
706-543-8113
www.redmulegrits.us
Grits

**New York City Community
Garden Coalition**
232 East 11th Street
New York, NY 10003
347-699-6099
www.nyccgc.org

Nora Mill Granary
7107 South Main Street
Helen, GA 30545
1-800-927-2375
www.noramill.com
Grits

Nordic Ware
1-877-466-7342
www.nordicware.com
Waffle irons and bakeware

Olive and Sinclair Chocolate
1628 Fatherland Street
Nashville, TN 37206
615-262-3007
www.oliveandsinclair.com
Chocolate

Oliver Farm
229-406-0906
www.oliverfarm.com
Pecan flour

Paisanos Meat Market
162 Smith Street
Brooklyn, NY 11201
718-855-2641
www.lospaisanosmeatmarket.com
Venison

Protein Plus
Fitzgerald, GA 31750
229-423-5528
www.proteinplusflour.com
Peanut flour

Sahadi's
187 Atlantic Avenue
Brooklyn, NY 11201
718-624-4550
www.sahadis.com
Dried fruits, nuts, zaatar

Saxelby Cheese
120 Essex Street
New York, NY 10002
212-228-8204
www.saxelbycheese.com

**Stony Brook
WholeHeartedFoods**
500 Technology Farm Drive
Geneva, NY 14456
1-877-292-8369
www.wholeheartedfoods.com
Squash seed oils

Sunrise Mart
494 Broome Street
New York, NY 10012
212-219-0033
www.sunrisemart-ny.com
Yuzu chili paste

Vitamix
1-800-848-2649
www.vitamix.com

Whisk
231 Bedford Avenue
Brooklyn, NY 11211
718-218-7230
www.whisknyc.com
Kitchen supplies

White Lily
1-800-595-1380
www.whitelily.com
All-purpose flour

With Love, From Brooklyn
718-399-3284
www.withlovefrombrooklyn.com
Mike's Hot Honey, Brooklyn Slate
cheese tray, Mast Brothers cacao
nibs

Acknowledgments

Living in New York City and having the opportunity to build a career around food and write a cookbook is a privilege. I owe a thank you to so many for this Up South journey. There are many names that show up on these pages and some I've overlooked—charge it to my head and not my heart.

Justin Schwartz and Anton Nocito were my two lucky charms early in this process, and your generosity will never go unnoticed.

On the top of the list is my literary agent, Sharon Bowers. Immediately, she believed in my entry into the publishing world, and I'm grateful.

I'm indebted to Ann Treistman, my editor at Countryman Press/W. W. Norton for never asking me to change my concept and graciously allowing my ideas to come alive. I need to acknowledge Sarah Bennett, editorial assistant, for stepping outside of her wordsmith world to navigate my tiny kitchen during the photo shoot.

Thanks must go to Noah Fecks. I'm beyond pleased with the photography and honored to work with a photographer I respect dearly! Hand claps for Greta Titelman and Clay Williams . . . you guys were great in assisting Noah.

Halfway through recipe testing Emily Hanhan helped me get organized and assisted me in the kitchen. Thank you for answering my late-night text messages and being my second set of taste buds.

I'm lucky to have had volunteer recipe testers who jumped into the process. Eryn Stutts, Jenn de la Vega, Jenn Cole, Jill Astmann Karol, Judy Shertzer, Kathy Blake, Kelly Vass, Misha McMurtray, Michele Washington, Nadine Nelson, Nora Chovanec, Patricia A. Patton, Tia Chriss, Wayne Suber . . . thanks for donating your time, cooking skills, and comments.

Shannon Mustipher is my right hand on most of my food projects. Without her influence, there would be no fried parsley with the chicken, fennel bulb usage, or a muscadine cocktail. I'm grateful for your influence and our collaborations.

It's Dr. Jessica B. Harris to many, but over the years it's just Jessica to me. Thank you kindly for writing the book's foreword. It's a true honor to know and love the high priestess of black foodways and culture. I treasure our yearly trek to Martha's Vineyard, Massachusetts, and the many peeks you've given me inside your lush life. Until the day I die, I'll remind the masses the path you have blazed for us all.

Bryant Terry . . . I value every text, e-mail, and nudge of encouragement. You ushered me into the new author club pretty well!

Sanura Weathers, Nancy McDermott, Michael Twitty . . . you put the icing on the cake, and I'm excited to have you as a part of my dream come true.

I need to give a shout-out to Heritage Radio Network. Because of you, I was able to spread my wings in the two shipping containers turned radio station in the garden of Roberta's pizza restaurant. Patrick

Martins, Jack Inslee, and Nat Weiner took a chance on me in 2009 and gave me a platform and the confidence needed to maneuver the food scene—salute!

There are many food colleagues who supported me during my "I can't attend because I'm working on the book" phase or were an inspiration through this process: Holley Atkinson, Dara Furlow, Therese Nelson, Donny Tsang, Frederick Opie, Toni Tipton-Martin, Amy Krawowitz, Nichelle Stephens, Nina Ichikawa, Charmaine Bee, Heather Watkins-Jones, Linda Pelaccio, Matt Timms, Jackie Gordon, Leda Meredith, Fany Gerson, Chitra Agrawal, David Campaniello, Gerardo Gonzalez, Nicholas Morgenstern, Adrian Miller, Jane Lerner, Autumn Giles, Elizabeth Stark, and Jocelyn Delk Adams.

There are a core group of friends who've endured countless dinner parties, reruns of dishes, expeditions to specialty shops and restaurants, and conversations about the highs and lows of writing a cookbook. Now back to our regular program . . . Moriba Jackson, Melissa Danielle, Leslie Ware, Kamau Ware, Sean Chriss, Jordan A. Colbert, Stacey N. West, Reginald Dye, Gabrielle Fulton Ponder, Greg Ponder, Anu Prestonia, Quinton Cameron, Joi Jackson, Zach Jackson, Adriana Velez, Adriane Stewart, Damian McCleod, Kamau Akabueze, Lynn Pitts, and Anne Pope.

Also, I want to thank my mama—Janis Marie Taylor Young—and two aunts, Joann and Sandra Taylor, for giving me space to soar and for their endless sacrifices. You ladies were always fine with me cooking full meals before I was a teenager.

Tammy Gartrell, Toni Lumpkin, Shirley Taylor, Marjorie Shorter-Horne—thanks for helping me during my photo digging and for providing family stories. Mattie Franks, Ann Franks, Antonio Franks, Rhonda Smith, Mark Smith, Cynthia Murrille, Jerel Matthews, Aisha Floyd, LaTonya Hortage . . . fortunate to have ya'll as the roots of my tree.

Finally, I'm sure this book wouldn't exist without the support of my husband, Adrian. He provides an energy that pushes me beyond the impossible and is my forever partner in chasing Dixie.

Index